The Love of Loves in the Song of Songs

"Phil Ryken is a master expositor of the Scripture, and he uses all his ability to beautifully unpack one of the most intriguing and difficult books of the Bible to understand—the Song of Solomon. Historically, interpreters have read the book as either/or. It is either about human romance or about our relationship with Jesus. Ryken reads the book as both/and—both in its immediate historical context (about romance) and its whole canonical context (about the spousal love of Jesus Christ.) And, of course, biblical wisdom about love and sexuality has perhaps never been as crucial and needed by the church as it is today. An important book for us all!"

Timothy C. Keller, Pastor Emeritus, Redeemer Presbyterian Church, New York City

"*The Love of Loves in the Song of Songs* is a book that every serious Bible student will want. A thoroughly researched, insightful, and challenging treatment of one of Scripture's most engaging and relevant books, written by one of our generation's finest pastoral theologians!"

J. D. Greear, author, *Not God Enough*; President, Southern Baptist Convention; Pastor, The Summit Church, Raleigh-Durham, North Carolina

"Our culture is deeply confused about sexuality and marriage. Not coincidentally, it is equally confused about the God who created humanity for a committed, exclusive, loving relationship with himself. This book shows us the remedy in the Song of Songs, the divine love song that shows us how our human marriages ought to work and how they ought to mirror Christ's passionate love for his bride. Ryken shows us how the song speaks to everyday relationships and, in doing so, how it points us to the One who made us for himself."

Iain M. Duguid, Professor of Old Testament, Westminster Theological Seminary; author, *Song of Songs* (Reformed Expository Commentary)

"Phil Ryken looks at this neglected book of the Bible, Song of Songs, on its own terms and with wonderful gospel awareness. He presents a truly thrilling vision of human sexuality along with the lover's heart of God himself. It has had a deep impact on me already, and I'd love for you to benefit from it too."

Sam Allberry, Speaker, Ravi Zacharias International Ministries; author, *Is God Anti-Gay?* and *7 Myths about Singleness*

"After reading *The Love of Loves in the Song of Songs*, I will never read this biblical book in the same way again. Ryken skillfully weaves into each passage God's wisdom about both the magnificence of human marriage and the romance of our redemption. I can't think of any Christian—single or married—who wouldn't benefit from this book."

Jani Ortlund, Executive Vice President, Renewal Ministries

"Here is a book of costly value for both single and married people! I have been blessed to read this, and through Ryken's exposition I see how the Word made flesh in the Song of Songs is brighter and more wonderful than I imagined. Ryken's call for obedience to Scripture's authority is convicting, but we are given hope and help as we read. He says that this Song 'operates simultaneously on at least two different levels,' teaching us about Christ with his bride, which speaks to what a truly godly marriage can be, and how all of us in the body, single or married, are his true bride."

Valerie Elliot Shepard, author, *Pilipinto's Happiness* and *Devotedly: The Personal Letters and Love Story of Jim and Elisabeth Elliot*

The Love of Loves in the Song of Songs

Philip G. Ryken

CROSSWAY®
WHEATON, ILLINOIS

The Love of Loves in the Song of Songs

Published by Crossway
1300 Crescent Street
Wheaton, Illinois 60187

Cover design: Connie Gabbert

First printing 2019

Printed in the United States of America

Trade paperback ISBN: 978-1-4335-6253-2
ePub ISBN: 978-1-4335-6256-3
PDF ISBN: 978-1-4335-6254-9
Mobipocket ISBN: 978-1-4335-6255-6

Library of Congress Cataloging-in-Publication Data

Names: Ryken, Philip Graham, 1966- author.
Title: The love of loves in the Song of songs / Philip G. Ryken.
Description: Wheaton, Illinois : Crossway, [2019] | Includes bibliographical references and index.
Identifiers: LCCN 2018019951 (print) | LCCN 2018042521 (ebook) | ISBN 9781433562549 (pdf) | ISBN 9781433562556 (mobi) | ISBN 9781433562563 (epub) | ISBN 9781433562532 (tp) | ISBN 9781433562563 (epub) | ISBN 9781433562556 (mobipocket)
Subjects: LCSH: Bible. Song of Solomon—Criticism, interpretation, etc.
Classification: LCC BS1485.52 (ebook) | LCC BS1485.52 .R95 2019 (print) | DDC 223/.907—dc23
LC record available at https://lccn.loc.gov/2018019951

Crossway is a publishing ministry of Good News Publishers.

VP 29 28 27 26 25 24 23 22 21 20 19
15 14 13 12 11 10 9 8 7 6 5 4 3 2 1

To Josh and Anna,
whose amazing love story is still being written,
and to the Savior who is also our Lover, our Friend

Contents

Prologue

I Love You Always, Forever

The woman slipped into the pew in front of me and sat down, alone, just a few minutes before the worship service began. I had never seen her before, although at College Church in Wheaton it is common to see people with Down syndrome. She stood up for the opening hymn and so together we sang, "Fairest Lord Jesus, Ruler of all nature, Son of God and Son of Man! Thee will I cherish, thee will I honor, thou, my soul's glory, joy, and crown."

What the woman did next caught me by surprise. She put down her worship folder, a little impatiently, as if somehow it was in the way. Then she sang the rest of the hymn from memory and at the same time used her hands to express its words in American Sign Language. She wanted to praise God with her whole person, body as well as soul.

As I watched, the woman's gestures made the words of the hymn come alive. I found myself walking through fair meadows and spring woodlands, or looking up at "the twinkling, starry host." Most of all, I could see the face of my beautiful Savior, Jesus Christ, whose hands were pierced for my transgressions.

As my spiritual sister gave glory and honor to the "Lord of all nations," her face was radiant, her visible words had a graceful beauty, and I had the unmistakable impression that she was deeply in love. Jesus Christ was the predominant passion of this woman's life. She was not "disabled," as some would say, but divinely empowered to worship. Nor was she single, as I had assumed from the absence of a ring on her finger. Rather, she was engaged to be married, for the beauty of her worship came from a heart that was betrothed to the Son of God.

This is the relationship that God wants to have with every one of us, male or female, married or single. He wants us to have an exclusive relationship, like the intense affection a bride has for the man she is preparing to marry, with the abiding security that comes from a groom who promises to be faithful unto death.

Introducing the Song of Songs

One of the best places to see a passionate, permanent love relationship is in the Bible's most famous love song—the ideal romance that we read about in the Song of Songs.

Admittedly, most books are easier to write about than the Song of Songs. To begin with, it is hard to know exactly how to connect the book's message with the life of King Solomon, who may or may not have been its author but is clearly mentioned in the first verse. Also, the Song of Songs is unashamed to talk about human sexuality, which some people find a little embarrassing. The book is "naked" in ways that some Christians wish they could cover up. Then there is the vexing question of how to relate the book's human relationship to the love that God wants to share with his people.

In spite of these difficulties, I have wanted to teach this book for a long time. One of the first sermons I ever preached came from chapter 2, with its thrilling exclamations: "My beloved is mine, and I am his" (v. 16); "He brought me to the banqueting house, and his banner over me was love" (v. 4). I got more serious about studying the Song of Songs when I visited the famous Bodmer Library on the shores of Lake Geneva in Switzerland. The Bodmer boasts one of the world's most extraordinary collections of ancient religious texts, biblical manuscripts, and other famous books. It is perhaps the best place in the world to see the religious and intellectual history of humanity.

There I saw a stunning manuscript of the Song of Songs from the early Middle Ages—the seventh century, as I recall. The colorful hand lettering was beautiful, but what really captured my attention was the expansive white space around the text. Obviously, the text had been copied by someone who knew how to read poetry. The words were not crammed onto the page the way they are in a two-column Bible but allowed to breathe. The scribe wanted each line of love poetry to be savored before moving on to the next. Seeing the book written out as a beautiful love poem awakened my desire to study it and then to preach it.

Not long afterward, I read the manuscript for a commentary on the Song of Songs by my friend Iain Duguid, who studied Old Testament at Cambridge before becoming my pastor when I was a theology student at Oxford. Professor Duguid has an exceptional ability to understand the Old Testament in connection to Christ and then apply its gospel message for everyday Christianity. The more I read his commentary—to which this little book is deeply indebted—the more I wanted to share the love of loves that we encounter in the Song of Songs.

Our culture needs this book. As a college president, I often hear students ask for more guidance in understanding human sexuality. They are not just looking for a list of biblical do's and don't's (although such a list may have its place); what they want to understand is the stunning beauty of God's design and his higher purpose for our romantic relationships. We live in a world where sexuality is ruined by sin, its beauty obscured by our brokenness. We need a divine vision for the way sex was meant to be, with a gospel that offers forgiveness for sexual sin and an empowering grace to live into the sexuality that God wants to give us. We also need a deeper understanding of the intimacy that God wants to have with each one of us and how that intimacy relates to our singleness or to our status as husbands and wives, as the case may be.

The best way to capture God's vision for anything is simply to work through some relevant part of the Bible, letting God's Spirit set the agenda through Scripture. When we turn to the Song of Songs, we encounter a love story told in the form of a love song that is part of the greatest love story ever told.

The Way We Were and Were Meant to Be

A good place to begin is by setting the Song of Songs in its wider context. I do not intend to treat the book like an allegory, in which everything in the book stands for something else, and in which we start coming up with meanings that the author never intended. But I do want to be faithful to God's purposes for marriage and romance, which the Bible consistently regards as mysteries that point beyond themselves to God's everlasting love. Whenever we talk about the way that a husband loves his wife, we are never simply talking about marriage; we are always talking about Christ's great love for the church (see Eph. 5:25–32). The sexual union of man and wife is not an allegory, strictly speaking, but it is analogous to the spiritual union that God shares with his people.

Thus the Bible repeatedly uses marriage as a metaphor for the divine-human love relationship. The Song of Songs becomes an important part of this pattern by putting the romance of our redemption into poetry and song. We might think of this book as the soundtrack for our love relationship with the living God.

The love story begins with the first man and the first woman, Adam and Eve. It was not good for the man to be alone. In order to fulfill God's purpose in the world—and for his own well-being—Adam needed an equal partner and complementary companion. So God made a woman. And then, as the father of the bride, he presented her to the man. When he saw her, Adam suddenly became a lyrical poet:

> This at last is bone of my bones
>   and flesh of my flesh;
> she shall be called Woman,
>   because she was taken out of Man. (Gen. 2:23)

The first human words in recorded history were expressed in the form of a love song, which the Bible immediately places in the wider context of marriage: "Therefore a man shall leave his father and his mother and hold fast to his wife, and they shall become one flesh" (Gen. 2:24). Forsaking all other human relationships—including the precious parental bond that first brought them into the world—a husband and wife are bound together in an exclusive union that is secured by promises of abiding love.

We are so familiar with this passage that sometimes we fail to see how astonishing it is. The Bible begins with the story of creation. God has been at work making a universe. Light shines in the darkness. Stars are scattered across immensities of space. Galaxies spin into place. Then, against the vast backdrop of a cosmos that is consecrated for the worship of God, we are introduced to one man and one woman who are joined in one marriage.

Adam and Eve are so small and insignificant that they are beneath anyone's notice—unless somehow their mutual love relationship is at the very heart of what God is doing in the entire universe. Ray Ortlund writes:

> The attention of the text shifts from the heavens and the earth coming together in cosmic order to a man and a woman coming together in earthly marriage. . . . There it is, this peculiar thing we call marriage, tenderly portrayed in its humble reality and delicate innocence against the enormous backdrop of the creation.[1]

In some mysterious way, with the union of this man and this woman, the curtain rises on the redemptive purposes of God.

What we discover as the story unfolds is that the one-flesh relationship of Adam and Eve is the divinely ordained pattern for marriage and also one of the Bible's primary pictures for God's relationship with his people. Isaiah said it as simply and as directly as he could. "Your Maker is your husband," spoke the prophet. And, "As the bridegroom rejoices over the bride, so shall your God rejoice over you" (Isa. 54:5; 62:5). Similarly, in the book of Jeremiah God identifies himself as Israel's husband, going back to the time of the exodus out of Egypt (Jer. 31:32).

This comparison is multidimensional, because divine and human marriage hold many things in common. Both relationships are based on love. Husbands and wives share mutual ties of intimate affection. So, too, God is in love with us, and we are in love with him, or at least we ought to be. Both relationships are bound by promises. Human marriage is rightly understood as a covenant, which is why every wedding has vows. The Bible uses similar language to describe our relationship with our Redeemer. God has made a covenant with us—a covenant of everlasting love (e.g., Deut. 7:9; Jer. 31:31–33). So we are betrothed to the God who says to us, "I love you always, forever."

Here is another similarity between divine and human marriage: both relationships are meant to be exclusive, inviolable. There are bonds of intimacy—especially sexual intimacy—that husbands and wives should never share with anyone else. In the same way, God rightly claims all of our honor, affection, and worship. When he says, "You shall have no other gods before me" (Ex. 20:3), he is saying, in effect, "Repeat after me: 'I, believer, take thee, Yahweh, to be my lawful wedded husband.'"

The exclusivity of this relationship explains why it is right and good for God to be jealous. *Jealousy* sounds like a bad word, but when it comes to marriage, jealousy has its place. When God says, "I the LORD your God am a jealous God" (e.g., Ex. 20:5), he is taking the part of a faithful husband who longs for his wife's loving embrace and thus refuses to share her love with anyone else. The Old Testament is the story of an exclusive love, in which God styles himself as the husband of his people.

When we turn to the New Testament, suddenly the groom walks into the room. His name is Jesus of Nazareth, also called the Christ, the Son of God. So when John the Baptist explained who he was in relation to Jesus, he called himself "the friend of the bridegroom, who . . . rejoices greatly at the bridegroom's voice" (John 3:29). This makes Jesus the bridegroom—the one who gives himself to the bride. Jesus sometimes used the same imagery to explain his saving work. He compared his kingdom to a king who throws a wedding feast for his son (Matt. 22:2) or to maidens waiting to meet the groom (Matt. 25:1).

Later, when the apostle Paul wanted to explain what Jesus had done to save his people, he said it was like a husband who loved his wife so much that he gave himself up for her (Eph. 5:25–27). Jesus is so in love with us that he was willing to do whatever it took to make us his bride. Like a valiant prince, he went out to slay that old dragon, Satan, which he did by dying a bloody death on the bloody hill of Calvary. By this reasoning, the cross is an expression of matrimonial affection—the sacrificial love of a doting husband for a beloved bride. Taken together, these passages show that marriage is not a superficial metaphor, but a sacred mystery that is introduced at the beginning of the world and lies close to the heart of the gospel. To quote again from Ray Ortlund, "Marriage from the beginning was meant to be a tiny social platform on which the love of Christ for his church and the church's responsiveness to him could be put on visible display."[2] Thus a faithful marriage is the gospel made visible to the watching world.

If we were to trace the full trajectory of this love story, we would arrive at a match made in heaven, celebrated at the last of all weddings (Rev. 19:7–9), when "a bride adorned for her husband" will come down from heaven and become "the wife of the Lamb" (Rev. 21:2, 9). We were made to be married to the Son of God—the fair prince who is waiting for us at "the marriage supper of the Lamb" (Rev. 19:9). Think of it this way: the Bible begins with a blind date (when Adam opens his eyes to see Eve) and ends with a wedding reception (where all of us get to dance with Jesus).

So the relationship that God wants to have with us is like the mutual affection of a man and a woman who are so deeply in love that they promise not to love anyone else but stay together for the rest of their lives. Whether we are married or single, all of us are invited into this spiritual marriage. This is why Adam and Eve were there at the beginning and why the Bible says that marriage should be held in honor by everyone (Heb. 13:4). We are all lovers—lovers who were always meant to be a pure bride for one husband (2 Cor. 11:2).

One of the most famous lines in English literature is the aside that Jane Eyre makes at the climactic moment of Charlotte Brontë's novel of the same name. After many disappointments in life and love, Jane is finally united with the man she loves, Edward Rochester. The final chapter thus begins with her immortal words: "Reader, I married him."[3] The storyline of the Bible comes to a similar climax in its closing chapters, when the Son of God finally is able to say this about the church: "Reader, I married her!"

But It's All Over Now

I wish I could say that in the romance of our redemption we have always had a perfect relationship, but we haven't. It is sad to say, but the majority of the passages in the Old Testament that use marital imagery to describe our relationship with God talk about marital failure. Again and again, God accuses his people of being unfaithful, of having casual idolatry and committing spiritual adultery, of "play[ing] the harlot" (Ps. 106:39 NKJV), of worshiping other gods in every city square (Ezek. 16:31), "on every high hill, and under every green tree" (Jer. 2:20). The Bible is not afraid to say that the wife of God has become a whore.[4]

What happens in Jeremiah 2 and 3 is especially shocking, for in these chapters God actually files for divorce. Giving legal testimony in a court of law, he starts at the beginning and goes back to their honeymoon, when Israel was young and in love: "I remember the devotion of your youth, your love as a bride" (Jer. 2:2). This was in the days when God rescued Israel from Egypt and led his people through the wilderness.

That was then, but this is now, and Israel is guilty of the great sin of spiritual adultery. So God files a covenant lawsuit: "I still contend with you," he says, using legal terminology (Jer. 2:9). Then he brings exhibit after exhibit of his people's unfaithfulness. One image is especially disturbing. God compares his people to "a wild donkey used to the wilderness, in her heat sniffing the wind! Who can restrain her lust? None who seek her need weary themselves; in her month they will find her" (Jer. 2:24). God's people have such a voracious appetite for worshiping other gods that they are like a donkey in heat, sniffing the wind, hoping to detect the scent of another sexual partner. This is what it is like when we say that God is not enough for us. Instead of walking with Jesus, we run to money, sex, and power or to cynicism and criticism and all the other idols that seduce us with the promise to satisfy us—a promise they will never keep.

What makes the Bible's sexually charged imagery especially apt is that Canaanite religion—such as Israel was tempted to practice—often was characterized by ritual prostitution. People went to the hilltop shrines of the pagan gods not merely to worship but especially to have sexual intercourse. Listen how graphically the Bible describes what God's people were doing:

> You have played the whore with many lovers. . . .
> Lift up your eyes to the bare heights, and see!
>   Where have you not been ravished?
> By the waysides you have sat awaiting lovers. . . .
> You have polluted the land
>   with your vile whoredom. (Jer. 3:1–2)

Simply put, God's people have been sleeping with other gods.

We find similar imagery in the book of Hosea, which begins with perhaps the strangest command that God ever gave to one of his prophets. He told Hosea to marry a prostitute. Why on earth would God do this? Because he wanted to give Israel a living object lesson of spiritual unfaithfulness. So he said: "Go, take to yourself a wife of whoredom and have children of whoredom, for the land commits great whoredom by forsaking the LORD" (Hos. 1:2). The point was that Israel was like Gomer: although God was her faithful husband, she wanted to be with other lovers.

Jeremiah and Hosea wanted people to see how disordered our desires are, how serious sin is, and how much damage this does to our love relationship with the living God. Every sin is a kind of spiritual adultery. Understand that any time we sin against God—whenever we are proud of our intellectual accomplishments, or worry about things that he tells us not to worry about, or minimize others so we can maximize ourselves, or give in to secret sexual temptation, or rely on our own strength rather than acknowledging our weakness, or commit any other sin—we are unfaithful to God. In every case, we are choosing not to love God but to love something else instead, which is the same thing as cheating on our divine spouse.

The Love That Will Not Let Us Go

Here is where the love story gets truly amazing, because you would think that God would walk away from us. Why would any husband put up with repeated unfaithfulness? If he knows that his virgin bride has become a brazen prostitute, then obviously he will follow through with the divorce, right?

Except that he doesn't. What God does instead is to go back to his people again and again. As an ardent lover, he tenderly wins us back to his love. He is always ready to renew his vows to us and for us to renew our vows to him.

God's love comes with a grace so powerful that it cleanses his people's sin and makes them pure again. Remember the wild donkey, sniffing the wind for another partner? Later in Jeremiah, God uses a very different image for his people and calls Israel a virgin. Humanly speaking, once you lose your virginity, you can never get it back. But the sanctifying power of God's forgiveness restores his people to perfect purity. By "the chemistry of grace,"[5] the faithless people of God are fully entitled to wear pure white on their wedding day (see Isa. 61:10; Eph. 5:26–27; Rev. 21:2). Such is the obvious symbolism of Christian weddings in the Western tradition; a white dress is a sign of virginal purity. Such purity is nothing that we can preserve; it is something that only God can produce. And he does:

> I have loved you with an everlasting love;
>   therefore I have continued my faithfulness to you.
> Again I will build you, and you shall be built,
>   O virgin Israel! (Jer. 31:3–4)

"Let us rejoice and exult
    and give him the glory,
for the marriage of the Lamb has come,
    and his Bride has made herself ready;
it was granted her to clothe herself
    with fine linen, bright and pure"—

for the fine linen is the righteous deeds of the saints. (Rev. 19:7–8)

Even when we do not love God, he is still in love with us. Even when we are guilty of sexual sin, there is grace for us. Even when we are unfaithful to God, he remains faithful to us. Thus Karl Barth rightly observed that in the Bible, "we have to reckon with the unfaithfulness of the wife, but never with the unfaithfulness of the Husband."[6]

We see the contrast between God's faithfulness and our unfaithfulness perhaps most graphically in the book of Hosea. The prophet marries a prostitute. Then she goes out and does what prostitutes do: she pursues other lovers (Hos. 2:7, 13). But God tells Hosea to go find her and bring her back home: "Go again, love a woman who . . . is an adulteress, even as the Lord loves the children of Israel, though they turn to other gods" (Hos. 3:1). By this point, Gomer must have been sold into slavery, because in order to bring her back home, Hosea has to buy her back. He ends up paying "fifteen shekels of silver and a homer and a lethech of barley" (Hos. 3:2), a price which suggests that he purchased her at auction. Gomer was sold to the highest bidder, who turned out to be the husband that she betrayed. Imagine paying the price for someone else's spiritual adultery!

But that is what this love story is all about. Look at Christ on the cross, and count the cost of your redemption. When Jesus died at Calvary, he was the Bridegroom paying the bride price. He was a wounded lover, pierced for our adulterous transgressions. He was dying to win us back to his love so that he could say the same thing to us that he said to Israel in the days of Hosea and Gomer: "I will betroth you to me forever. I will betroth you to me in righteousness and in justice, in steadfast love and in mercy. I will betroth you to me in faithfulness. And you shall know the LORD" (Hos. 2:19–20).

The Song of Songs is part of this remarkable story. The song that is sung in its pages "echoes the melody of another deeper and richer song, a song about a true and faithful Lover who is not like Solomon, with his massive harem of disposable women, but rather One who loves and gives himself for his bride."[7]

We have been unfaithful in every way. This is true individually and also corporately. Is there any sin we have not committed? Pride, jealousy, slander, selfish ambition, lust, adultery, greed, racism, anger, idolatry—the list goes on and on. Every one of these sins is a form of spiritual unfaithfulness to the Son of God.

We are so unfaithful. But God loves us with an everlasting love. Therefore, he continues his faithfulness to us. Jesus Christ is the loving groom who takes us into his loving arms and says, "I love you always, forever." This undeserved romance is the ultimate reality. Even after everything we have done wrong, we are still betrothed to the Son of God. So we should love accordingly, pursuing spiritual chastity as we wait in hope for the return of our beloved Bridegroom.

One college student experienced God's holy love in a deeply personal way when she stood up to give her testimony at an impromptu evening worship service where many students were confessing their sins. She told the Lord that she was fully present and then felt prompted to confess her guilt and her hope before what she described as "a crowd of faces both recognizable and unrecognizable." As she encountered the Lord that night, she heard the words tumble out of her mouth: "When we say yes to an exclusive relationship with God, we, by default, say no to every other lover." She continued, "I am guilty of idols; I am guilty of sexual sin." In that moment of genuine contrition she was overcome by the Lord's glory and sensed his loving mercy speaking to her broken heart, "I am pleased with you. I love you."

What God said to that college student is what he says to all of his beloved, broken people: "I love you always, forever."

1

You're the One That I Want

The Song of Songs, which is Solomon's.

Let him kiss me with the kisses of his mouth!
For your love is better than wine;
  your anointing oils are fragrant;
your name is oil poured out;
  therefore virgins love you.
Draw me after you; let us run.
  The king has brought me into his chambers.

We will exult and rejoice in you;
  we will extol your love more than wine;
  rightly do they love you.

I am very dark, but lovely,
  O daughters of Jerusalem,
like the tents of Kedar,
  like the curtains of Solomon.
Do not gaze at me because I am dark,
  because the sun has looked upon me.
My mother's sons were angry with me;
  they made me keeper of the vineyards,
  but my own vineyard I have not kept!
Tell me, you whom my soul loves,

where you pasture your flock,
where you make it lie down at noon;
for why should I be like one who veils herself
beside the flocks of your companions?

If you do not know,
O most beautiful among women,
follow in the tracks of the flock,
and pasture your young goats
beside the shepherds' tents.

I compare you, my love,
to a mare among Pharaoh's chariots.
Your cheeks are lovely with ornaments,
your neck with strings of jewels.

We will make for you ornaments of gold,
studded with silver.

While the king was on his couch,
my nard gave forth its fragrance.
My beloved is to me a sachet of myrrh
that lies between my breasts.
My beloved is to me a cluster of henna blossoms
in the vineyards of Engedi. (Song 1:1–14)

Picture the scene. A teenage girl is engaged to be married to a young man from her village somewhere on the outskirts of Jerusalem. After a period of formal betrothal, the bride price has been paid, and the couple is eager to join in holy matrimony. The smell of fresh meat rises from an open flame—goat meat, perhaps, or maybe even a fatted calf. The entire community comes out to witness the sacred vows and then to celebrate with the happy couple and their proud families. The wedding feast will last for an entire week—seven days of singing and dancing.

As the festivities begin, skilled musicians tune their instruments, and a soloist begins to sing a familiar melody. Her voice gives public expression to the bride's passionate love, soon to be consummated in the privacy of the wedding chamber:

> Let him kiss me with the kisses of his mouth!
> For your love is better than wine;
>   your anointing oils are fragrant;
> Your name is oil poured out;
>   therefore virgins love you. (Song 1:2–3)

A bridal chorus takes up the happy refrain: "We will exult and rejoice in you; we will extol your love more than wine; rightly do they love you" (Song 1:4). Then a male voice returns to the melody and sings, "O most beautiful among women. . . . Your cheeks are lovely with ornaments, your neck with strings of jewels" (Song 1:8, 10).

The scene we have just imagined is the most likely setting for the Song of Songs. Weddings in ancient Israel lasted as long as a week, and singing was always part of the festivities. From its presence in Holy Scripture, we may infer that the Song of Songs was at the top of the charts in those days. What wedding would be complete without it? For the people of God, singing these popular, emotional songs expressed a communal vision for marriage.

Prelude to the Song of Songs

These superlative lyrics were written by King Solomon—or were they? The phrasing of the title, which reads, "The

Song of Songs, which is Solomon's" (Song 1:1), may indicate that Solomon is the author, but it might just mean that the song was dedicated to him or in some other way associated with him.

If Solomon is the author—after all, we know that he wrote more than a thousand songs (1 Kings 4:32)—then he must be telling us to do as he says, not what he did. I say this because the Song of Songs is all about an exclusive relationship between one man and one woman, yet we know that King Solomon married seven hundred wives and had three hundred concubines (1 Kings 11:3). So if this is his book, he must have been writing with the chastened wisdom of his later years, when he finally realized what a massive mistake he had made by not being a one-woman man.

The perspective of this book contrasts sharply with Solomon's life experience in many ways. Rather than seeing sex as a conquest and marriage as a political alliance (see 1 Kings 11), the Song of Songs views marriage as a romance and sex as the seal of a sacred covenant. The author—whoever he was—dedicated his song to Solomon in order to cast a divine vision for marriage that stood against the idolatries of his contemporary culture.

This biblical song can do the same thing for us. We live in a culture that believes every desire should be satisfied. The Song of Songs aches with sexual desire, but it surrenders sex to the glory of God by securing the satisfaction of its desire within the bridal chamber. Pico Iyer was right when he said that this book "presents us with the taste of love, unfootnoted—and asks us to unlock the door according to our purity."[1] Our culture impatiently pushes past the erotic to experience the pornographic. By contrast, the Song of Songs presents adult themes with parental guidance. Its language is often sexually provocative but never spiritually impure.

To preserve this purity, we need to read the book in its proper context: covenant matrimony. The Song of Songs is not just *Solomon on Sex*, to borrow the title of one recent commentary. Instead, it is about sacred marriage and therefore about chastity, from beginning to end. We will encounter bridal imagery and marital vocabulary frequently in this book, especially in chapters 4 and 5. We will also hear people recite wedding vows (e.g., Song 2:16; 8:6). Understand, too, that marriage is the only context in which God-fearing people would have celebrated sex in ancient Israel. They understood—as not everyone in our culture does—that only covenant matrimony provides enough relational safety for our sexuality to be released in all its soul-bonding power. All of this leads Doug O'Donnell to conclude that the Song of Songs is "erotic poetry set within the ethical limits of the marriage bed."[2]

The word *poetry* is also important for knowing how to approach this book. A love song is simply a love poem set to music. So we need to read the Song of Songs poetically. This may seem intimidating to people who think they don't like poetry and say they have a hard time reading it. But in fact most people encounter love poems every day through listening to popular music. The love songs we listen to are really poems set to music. Like the Song of Songs, most of them have something to do with love, and sometimes sex. Their words have a way of getting inside us and connecting with our life experience, which explains why people often put song lyrics on their profile pages.

Thinking of the Song of Songs as a love song makes the book more accessible than we might at first think. Read this book the way you read the liner notes to an album of love songs. And listen to its message like you would listen to the playlist for the dance at a wedding reception. If we read the Song of Songs like a short story, we will be frustrated by its lack of clarity. But if we read this book the way it was meant to be read—as a loose collection of love songs from a steamy romance that became a happy marriage—we will enter into its joy.

The Woman's Desire

The song begins with a breathless desire: "Let him kiss me with the kisses of his mouth!" (Song 1:2). Did I mention yet that this is the hottest book in the Bible? The opening verse states the book's title. Then in the second verse we meet a woman who is smoldering. We don't know her name. We don't know the object of her desire. We don't know if her love is reciprocated or whether it will ever be consummated. Maybe the man she loves doesn't even know that she exists—it's just a crush from afar. But as far as she is concerned, this is love at first sight. Suddenly, the woman is in love.

Her impatience for passion is evident from the rapid progression in verses 2 to 4 from the third person ("Let him kiss me") to the second person ("Draw me after you") to the first-person plural ("Let us run"). She wants to be with the man she loves, so she is impatient for this relationship to move forward as fast as possible.

The woman's flaming passion is evident not only from the pronouns she uses but also from the nouns and verbs. Maybe it seems redundant for her to say that she wants the kisses "of his mouth." But in the ancient Near East, nose kisses were sometimes exchanged as a greeting of friendship.[3] So this woman wants to be clear: she is looking for a lover, not just a friend. She finds her beloved's fragrance irresistible—as in one of those cologne commercials where the man walks by and the women swoon. And when she says that his "love is better than wine" (1:2), the word she uses for her intoxicating attraction is a word for lovemaking.[4] Understand that this woman's goal is not to have a Bible study with the man she loves or simply to share an evening with him out on the town. It's "kisses" she wants—in the plural. Her vision for this relationship clearly ends with him carrying her across the threshold and into the bedroom—his royal chamber (1:4, 12). Needless to say, the woman is looking forward to their wedding night.

We are only a few verses into the Song of Songs and already we can understand why some rabbis warned the young men in their synagogues not to read this book until they turned thirty.[5] This is a book "about desire from beginning to end—desire stirred, desire frustrated, desire satisfied, desire frustrated again—but above all, desire."[6] One pastor I know likes to guide his parishioners by asking them probing questions about their desires: What do you want? How are you trying to get it? How is that working out for you? The Song of Songs asks us similarly probing questions about our sexual desire, which is one of God's good gifts, but like all good gifts it can be turned to sinful purposes. This makes the Song of Songs a perilous book for us to read. In bringing us close to ecstasy, it also draws us near to danger.

We should proceed with caution, therefore, and one of the best ways for us to be careful is to read the words of this book as closely as we can. At first, the woman's poetic language may seem over the top, but recognize that her affection is more than a shallow infatuation. In verse 3 she tells us that her lover's "name is oil poured out." Typically, when people fall in love, they love to hear the name of their beloved. The Ryken family has an old Scrabble set that my mother must have used right after she got engaged to my father, because her new name is written over and over again on the underside of the box top: Mary Alice Graham *Ryken*.

The woman in the Song of Songs is doing something even more significant. In biblical terms, a "name" is a reputation. So when she says that her lover's name is like sweet perfume and that all the maidens love him too, she is praising his character. She loves him for who he is, not just because he smells nice or because she imagines that he might be a good kisser. She loves everything about him.

Apparently, her friends agree. In verse 4 a choir of young virgins called "the daughters of Jerusalem"—think of them as bridesmaids or debutantes—pronounce their benediction on the man of her dreams, and on her desire for the consummation of their marriage: "We will exult and rejoice in you; we will extol your love more than wine; rightly do they love you." Later these young women will assist the wedding preparations by making "ornaments of gold, studded with silver" (1:11). As single women, they too have a vital interest in the success of their friend's marriage.

None of this quite fits our conventional categories for romance. Is the would-be bride a feminist or a traditionalist? It is hard to say. She boldly declares her affection for someone she loves and openly communicates her desires, including sexual desires. Yet at the same time she expects and longs for the man to provide leadership in their relationship. Notice that she wants *him* to kiss her (1:2), and also that she calls him her "king" (1:4, 12). In presenting this portrait of love and desire, the Bible is not bound by cultural constructs for gender but is helping us understand God's design for human relationships. Taking all of this into account, here is how Iain Duguid describes the dynamic partnership that we read about in this book: "In the Song, the woman is not a land to be conquered by the man or a field to be planted with his seed; she is a vineyard to be cultivated by him so that together they can enjoy the sweet wine of their relationship."[7]

Consider another paradox. The woman is independent enough to have desires of her own and then pursue them. She knows what she wants in a man. She also happens to know which man she wants. But she will only pursue this relationship with the support of her faith community. She wants the people around her—especially godly women—to bless and celebrate this relationship, which is not exclusively private but inclusively public.

Already we see signs of a healthy relationship: the woman will enter this partnership with equal passion, hoping and expecting to find a man who is strong enough to lead. And as their relationship develops, they will not cut themselves off from others; they will find strength in the counsel of their community.

The Woman's Hesitation

There is a problem, however, as there always seems to be when it comes to love and romance. The problem in this case is as old as sin and as current as today's fashion magazines. The woman is self-conscious about her physical appearance. "I am very dark, but lovely," she tells her friends. By way of comparison, she says that her skin is dark and coarse "like the tents of Kedar" (1:5). Then she explains why. It is because she has been working outdoors:

Do not gaze at me because I am dark,
because the sun has looked upon me,
My mother's sons were angry with me;
they made me keeper of the vineyards,
but my own vineyard I have not kept! (1:6)

To be clear, these verses are not about ethnicity. The Song of Songs does not put a biblical value judgment on a particular skin tone. It simply reflects the beauty standards of a culture in which wealthy people typically stayed indoors and poor people were darkened by the sun. The issue is social, not racial. In effect, the Song of Songs tells a Cinderella story. The heroine's brothers (or perhaps step-brothers, since she calls them "the sons of my mother") have forced her to work out in the fields, under the blazing sun. As a result, she has been too busy taking care of her family's vineyard to tend to her own complexion. So rather than thanking God that she's a country girl, she laments her rustic upbringing. Although she believed that she was attractive, she also worried about measuring up to her culture's standards for feminine beauty.

The Bible is realistic about the struggle we have with our embodiment. The burdens that many women carry because of body image are immense. Although standards may vary from culture to culture, there always seems to be something for a woman to try to improve: get a tan or else use skin cream to make your skin lighter; make your hair straight or else curl it; get your body flatter or make it curvier—there is always some feature that ought to be bigger, or smaller, or downright more beautiful than it is. Many men face similar struggles with their physiques, of course.

The anxiety and anguish of these cultural pressures came home to me one day when I was listening to the radio and heard an actress say that she was afraid to go out in public because she knew that she would never look as good as she looked in the movies, where every flaw was concealed. She hated to leave her house and go places where people would take her picture and perhaps make unflattering comments about her. At the time, she would have been on everyone's short list of the world's most beautiful people. But apparently she wasn't beautiful enough to look like herself! I was brokenhearted when I heard this, because I understood that our culture was holding the women I love—my wife and sisters, daughters and nieces—to a standard that no woman could ever meet, not even the most beautiful women in the world.

In her inner turmoil about her physical appearance, the woman in the Song of Songs reached out to the man she loved—the man she hoped would also love her:

> Tell me, you whom my soul loves,
> where you pasture your flock,
> where you make it lie down at noon;
> for why should I be like one who veils herself
> beside the flocks of your companions? (1:7)

Here the woman reveals a desire much deeper than kisses and cologne—a passion more intense than wanting to be carried across the threshold and into the king's bedchamber. She wants to know where she can go and be with the man she loves, not only at night but also during the daytime. In spite of her fears, she wants to see him face-to-face. In a word, she wants intimacy. Furthermore, she expresses this explicitly as something she wants with her soul, not just her body. Don't miss the deepest longing of the Song of Songs: not a sexual partner, but a soulmate.

The Man's Affirmation

Notice how the man responds. He finally speaks—the man whose love is better than wine and whose name is like sweet perfume. He does not let the woman's love go unrequited but responds directly and protectively to her insecurities. He tells the woman where she can find him, openly inviting her to spend time with him. And as he does so, he affirms her beauty:

> If you do not know,
>   O most beautiful among women,
> follow in the tracks of the flock,
>   and pasture your young goats
>   beside the shepherds' tents. (1:8)

This invitation falls somewhere between a guy asking a girl out on a date and inviting her to hang out with his friends. But notice how he begins: by praising her unadorned beauty. Notice, as well, how he does it. Obviously he is responding to her concerns about her complexion. But he is careful not to evaluate any and every part of her anatomy. He simply declares that she is beautiful, which may include her physical appearance but is not limited to that. Then he reinforces his compliment with a comparison:

> I compare you, my love,
>   to a mare among Pharaoh's chariots.
> Your cheeks are lovely with ornaments,
>   your neck with strings of jewels. (1:9–10)

A man should always be careful about comparing a woman to a horse, but in this case the guy probably got away with it. After all, a thoroughbred is one of the most beautiful animals that God ever created. But the point of this particular comparison is not simply the horse, but also the horse's adornment. What the man has in mind is one of the mares from Pharaoh's stables, dressed for a parade or some other ceremonial occasion. He compares the horse's ornately decorated bridle to the jewelry that his beloved wears.

Somehow it seems significant that at this stage of the song the man keeps his comments above the woman's neckline. He refers only to her face, and even there he is subtle, because he talks only about her jewelry. He notices how the woman—soon to be his bride—has enhanced her beauty. Her status as bride is clearly implied, for in ancient Israel jewelry was not for everyday use; it was mainly used at weddings.[8]

The practical application of these verses is not only for grooms who love their brides or limited to husbands who love their wives. Like most of what we read in Solomon's song, it has implications for single people as well as married people. It is for every godly man who wants to bless any woman who is made in the image of God.

When most young men talk about women, they make a lot of comments about their physical appearance, and a fair number of those comments are critical. But what would happen if Christian men said, "I refuse to criticize my sisters, and I won't let anyone else criticize them either"? What would happen if instead of seeing all the ways that women fail to measure up to some cultural standard of physical beauty that no one can meet anyway, men truly saw the total beauty of the women in their lives and then built them up with words of praise? When men recognize the gifts of women, respect their intellect, admire their character, affirm the dignity of their unique design, and then express this verbally, their sisters are empowered to become more completely the women that God is calling them to become.

Then take this one step farther. What if single Christian men took initiative to invite their sisters in Christ into meaningful relationships? This would do something more than improve the dating scene—although that would surely happen. More importantly, and more powerfully, it would bring genuine intimacy into everyday Christian relationships. Leave romance out of it for a moment: when men and women pursue open, caring, mutually respectful friendships and take time for deeper conversations, they strengthen one another for effective service in the kingdom of God.

This opportunity—this responsibility—is not just for men. It is also for Christian women. All of us can pursue greater intimacy in Christian friendships. But the example in Song of Songs 1 is for men especially. Christian men are called to look for the true beauty in every woman, to choose affirmation over criticism or comparison, and to pursue godly spiritual friendship.

The Mystery of Spiritual Matrimony

All of this takes on deeper significance when we draw a comparison to our relationship with Jesus Christ. Remember the wider context. The Song of Songs paints an idealized picture of any man and woman in love, or at least of a godly man and a godly woman who put their love for one another in the context of marriage as part of their surrender to God. But this picture is painted on a larger canvas. The Bible repeatedly uses marital imagery to describe God's love relationship with his people. The story of Adam and Eve in the garden of Eden is the trailer for an epic romance that ends with the Son of God marrying his beautiful bride, the church.

The Song of Songs is the soundtrack for that story. Its love is not merely human but also divine. This does not mean that we should treat the book as an allegory in which everything stands for something else, like some sort of secret code. Perhaps the most famous example of this approach comes from Cyril of Alexandria, who (among other things) claimed that when the Song compares the beloved to "a sachet of myrrh that lies between [two] breasts" (1:13), this refers to "Christ in the soul of the believer, who lies between the two great commands to love God and one's neighbor."[9] We should have sympathy for preachers who have read the Song of Songs this way—especially Bernard, who delivered eighty-six sermons on this book to the chaste and perhaps astonished monks of Clairvaux.[10]

The Song of Songs is not an allegory, but it is part of a bigger mystery—the mystery of the Father's love in Jesus Christ for his beloved and beautiful bride. So the song is not just about a man who loves a woman. It is also about the love of all loves, which means that there is a place in this story for all of us. The image of the bride is in the Bible to show "the uninhibited joy and tender intimacy of the divine-human communion" that all of us are offered through the Son of God."[11] One old rabbi described the Song of Songs as "a lock for which the key had been lost."[12] But the key has not been lost: the key is the revelation of Jesus Christ as the loving husband of the people of God.

Jesus wants to share his love with every one of us, whether we are male or female, married or single. By the grace of God, we discover that his name is oil poured out, and his cross is the fragrance of salvation (Eph. 5:2). We were made beautiful, yet we hesitate because we know our lives are darkened by sin, including all of the disordered desires of our broken sexuality. But God's affirmation to us is the gospel, which declares that

Jesus loves us and gave himself up for us (Eph. 5:25). This romance is the ultimate reality.

Now Jesus wants to satisfy our soul's desire to be intimate with the living God. The Savior who himself is altogether lovely intends to make us more beautiful than we can possibly imagine. With this purpose in mind, he has gone to prepare a place where we can go and be with him forever.

As we hope for his presence—with a longing for love that the Holy Spirit may intensify until it becomes an aching desire—we tell everyone we can that we have found the One that we want, the One who loves us most of all. And like the beloved woman in the Song of Songs, we join the people of God in celebrating his undying affection: "We will exult and rejoice in you; we will extol your love" (Song 1:4).

2

Underneath the Apple Tree

Behold, you are beautiful, my love;
behold, you are beautiful;
your eyes are doves.

Behold, you are beautiful, my beloved, truly delightful.
Our couch is green;
the beams of our house are cedar;
our rafters are pine.

I am a rose of Sharon,
a lily of the valleys.

As a lily among brambles,
so is my love among the young women.

As an apple tree among the trees of the forest,
so is my beloved among the young men.
With great delight I sat in his shadow,
and his fruit was sweet to my taste.
He brought me to the banqueting house,
and his banner over me was love.
Sustain me with raisins;
refresh me with apples,
for I am sick with love.

His left hand is under my head,
    and his right hand embraces me!
I adjure you, O daughters of Jerusalem,
    by the gazelles or the does of the field,
that you not stir up or awaken love
    until it pleases. (Song 1:15–2:7)

Starting with the church fathers—and then through the Middle Ages and up to the Puritans—the Song of Songs was one of the Bible's most popular books. Believe it or not, pastors preached and scholars commented on this book more than any other book in the Bible.[1] Why was this?

If you think the Song of Songs was popular because it is about sex, then you might be right. Maybe the venerable theologians of the early and medieval church were curious about human anatomy. Or maybe they were thrilled instead by the book's allegorical possibilities—the way its images could be interpreted to mean almost anything, which gave them unlimited opportunities to display their hermeneutical skills. After all, pastors and priests had to find some way of making the book appropriate to read in church. Nicholas of Lyra was not the only Bible scholar who thought that the Song of Songs had "a certain dishonorable and improper quality about it" unless it could be read allegorically.[2]

But I think something deeper was at work. We were made to be lovers, and this song awakens a desire for intimacy that can be satisfied only by a personal relationship with the living God. Our deep need for God's love explains why Christians have turned to this book repeatedly over the centuries, and why we still need to read it today.

Spiritually speaking, most of us live as if we were single rather than married. Married people always have to give some consideration to their spouses, whereas single people have much more control of their time, their money, and their life decisions, both big and small. Unfortunately, this is the way that many of us operate spiritually. Occasionally we remember that we are betrothed to Jesus Christ, the Bridegroom of heaven. But most of the time we operate independently. We are too busy with our own agenda to make much time for Jesus—like the student who says that he or she is too busy studying to have a girlfriend or a boyfriend. Pastor Iain Duguid challenges our priorities and invites our repentance:

> If you are married to Christ, is that relationship the center of your thinking? Do you find yourself dreaming about him, lost in amazement at how wonderful Christ is, how incredible it is that he should love you, and longing for more of his presence? Do you constantly wear out your friends and relations with your endless chatter about how wonderful your Beloved is? If you are anything like me, the answer most of the time is "No." I have to admit to living most of the time as a functional single, spiritually speaking. Every now and then I bump into Christ, as it were, and am reminded that we are married. . . . Much of the time I am so absorbed with my own earthly desires and projects that I admit to my shame that he never even crosses my mind.[3]

Jesus is calling out to us for a closer connection. When Saint Augustine finally realized what Jesus had to offer, he lamented all the time that he had wasted by living for himself. "Late it was that I loved you, beauty so ancient and so new," he said, "late I loved you!" Faith in Christ came later for Augustine, but not too late. As he looked back, he realized that Jesus had been pursuing him all along and that this was the love he had been longing for all his life: "You called, you cried out, you shattered my deafness: you flashed, you shone, you scattered my blindness: you breathed perfume, and I drew in my breath and I pant for you: I tasted and I am hungry and thirsty: you touched me, and I burned for your peace."[4]

Are you able to relate (even a little bit) to Augustine's spiritual passion? My reason for asking is that a desire for loving intimacy with Jesus Christ is one of the best indicators of our overall spiritual health.[5] If our love is growing cold, then the Song of Songs can help. As this book moves from unfulfilled desire to desire (partially) satisfied, it teaches us a good deal about love relationships at the human level. But it also reveals our greater and deeper hunger for the love of God, which can only be satisfied in the beautiful person of Jesus Christ.

An Eye for Beauty

When last we left our two young lovers, the fragrance of their affection lingered in the air like the memory of a stolen kiss. The woman imagined her beloved catching the scent of her sweet perfume (Song 1:12). Then she imagined holding him close, like the sachet of myrrh she kept concealed in her blouse (1:13), or like a bouquet of flowers clutched close to her bosom (1:14).

Suddenly they are together, standing face-to-face and speaking words of tender affection. This gives a chance for their relationship to grow the only way a romance can: through emotionally intimate conversations in which they build each other up by explicitly declaring their love for each other.

First, the man speaks (we know this from the gender pronouns in the original Hebrew text): "Behold, you are beautiful, my love; behold, you are beautiful; your eyes are doves" (1:15). The beloved tells her how beautiful she is, and then he says it again: "Wow! You look beautiful!" Some guys think they need to be clever, but simply telling a woman how beautiful she is—and saying it again—can go a long way. Then he gazed into her eyes and drew a comparison to the natural world: her eyes were pure and beautiful, like two doves.

Apparently, this woman's eyes really were the window to her soul, because she looked back at him and responded with terms of her own endearment: "Behold, you are beautiful, my beloved, truly delightful" (1:16).

As the Bible allows us to eavesdrop on these two lovers, I am reminded of the video I saw at a rehearsal dinner the night before the wedding of two students from Wheaton College. The groom's roommates had interviewed him on camera right before he went over to her dorm to ask her out on a date for the first time (somehow they had the feeling that she was "the one"). Then they hid in the bushes outside the lobby to film the "big ask" secretly. Their comments on the soundtrack were hilarious, especially when they told the couple's future children that they were recording everything for their benefit. The only thing the videographers couldn't capture was the couple's conversation; they were too far away. Fortunately, the Song of Songs takes us much closer, and as we listen to this dialogue, there is a lot for us to learn.

First, we learn the God-given power of mutual attraction. Chemistry is crucial to any romance. To say this is not unspiritual; it is simply to acknowledge the way that God made us. For a relationship to grow in the direction of godly marriage, a man and a woman must see what is beautiful in one another, both outwardly and inwardly. The beauty they see does not have to meet the perhaps unreasonable standards of their culture. It does not have to be seen by anyone else at all. And they don't have to see it the first time they meet, either. Often our awareness of someone's beauty grows over time. It can even come as an answer to prayer: "Lord, I see the possibility for a relationship here; give me the eyes to see his or her true beauty." But in the end, physical attraction and sexual desire are essential to a happy marriage.

We also learn how important it is for lovers to declare their affections. I remember going to see my father when I was a freshman in college to get the first and maybe the only romantic advice he ever gave me. I had fallen hard for Lisa Maxwell, but she still wasn't sure about me (understandably enough), and I didn't know what to do. "Do you love her?" my father asked. It didn't take me more than a few seconds to say, "Yes, I think I do." "Well," my father said, "you'd better tell her." I waited for more, but that's all he had to say (and, as it turned out, that was all I needed to hear).

The man in the Song of Songs had taken the same advice to heart. He had listened to the kind of wise counsel that the singer-songwriter Billy Joel gave in one of his most popular ballads: "Tell her about it / Tell her everything you feel / Give her every reason to accept / That you're for real."[6] Throughout this book the man repeatedly calls the woman his "love"—his darling, his sweetheart.

The woman he loved needed to hear this over and over again because she was vulnerable to an old insecurity: sometimes she found it hard to believe that she was very beautiful at all. We catch a hint of this when she says, "I am a rose of Sharon, a lily of the valleys" (2:1). Remember that she's a country girl who used to work out in the fields. So by talking about a flower out in the countryside, she was drawing an apt comparison. Her poetry may lead us to think that she was confident about her appearance. But a rose of Sharon or lily of the valley is merely a common desert wildflower—the kind of plant that may be somewhat beautiful, but also happens to be extremely common. Thus the woman was being self-deprecating. Perhaps the best contemporary comparison would be something like this: "I am a dandelion on the soccer field."

The woman was not fishing for a compliment here. Hesitantly, she was beginning to trust her beloved and to accept his admiration. But she wasn't ready to sing "I Feel Pretty" the way that Maria does in *West Side Story*.[7] She was somewhere between thinking of herself as rather plain and starting to believe that she could be beautiful to the man she loved.

Her beloved's response is perfect. It is witty, whimsical, and deeply affirming. The man says, "As a lily among the brambles, so is my love [there he goes again] among the young women" (2:2). He starts where she is. "You call yourself a wildflower," he says. "Okay, I can go along with that, but compared to everyone else, you're like a rare wildflower surrounded by common weeds." In English we say it like this: "You're a rose between two thorns."

The man in the Song of Songs sees the simple beauty in the woman he loves—the unique and God-given beauty that only she possesses—and then he praises her for it. After all, even the most common wildflower has uncommon beauty. Field lilies were so beautiful that they found a home in Solomon's temple, where they were sculpted around the basin for cleansing and decorated the tops of the great pillars (see 1 Kings 7:22, 26). Jesus saw their beauty too: when he asked his disciples to "consider the lilies of the field," he told them that "even

Solomon in all his glory was not arrayed like one of these" (see Matt. 6:28–29). The man in the Song of Songs saw exceptional beauty in the woman he loved and wisely used the image of a wildflower to praise her for it.

The Kind of Man to Look For

The woman saw his beauty, too, but she was looking for a lot more. Notice the transition she makes in chapter 1, verses 16 and 17, where "she moves almost impatiently beyond discussing his good looks to speak of their future together as a couple."[8] First she repeats his words back to him, nearly verbatim: "Behold, you are beautiful, my beloved." But then she describes the kind of home she hopes they can make together (notice how quickly her pronouns move from the second-person singular to the first-person plural—from "you" to "our"): "Our couch is green; the beams of our house are cedar; our rafters are pine."

At this point, some guys probably think that this is exactly what is wrong with some of the young women they meet: ask them out on a date, and they start planning what kind of house you'll live in when you get married and start a family! But don't miss the deeper significance of this woman's desire: her heart is longing for a home. She wants to live with her beloved, and so she imagines the home that they will build together—a beautiful house with strong beams.

A longing for home is one of our heart's deepest desires, whether we know it or not. We were made to find a permanent residence with the Father's only Son, the Bridegroom, Jesus Christ, who has made a solemn vow and joyful promise to go and prepare a place for us in his Father's mansions (see John 14:2). We are reminded of this hope for an eternal home every time a woman dreams about making a home with the man she loves and every time her beloved works to make her dream home a reality.

We see this dynamic at work on the television shows where couples are trying to find a new house. Usually the husband and the wife have somewhat different priorities and end up disagreeing about which house they like the best. But when it comes time to make a final decision, the man almost always defers. Why is this? Maybe it is because the woman's desire to make a home runs so deep.

This was certainly true of the woman in the Song of Songs. Her heart was looking for a home. Her beloved wisely recognized this and made a safe space for their relationship to grow. He protected her without ever patronizing her or seeing her as anything except his equal. Listen to the praise she gives him in response:

> As an apple tree among the trees of the forest,
> so is my beloved among the young men.
> With great delight I sat in his shadow,
> and his fruit was sweet to my taste.
> He brought me to the banqueting house,
> and his banner over me was love.
> Sustain me with raisins;
> refresh me with apples,
> for I am sick with love.
> His left hand is under my head,
> and his right hand embraces me! (2:3–6)

These verses tell us what this woman was looking for—and what many women are looking for—in a man. We already know that she thinks he's good looking. Now she uses vivid comparisons to describe some of his other attributes.

Her beloved is like an apple tree. Apple trees are strong, especially in a desert climate. They offer protective shade from the heat of the day; remember that this poor girl had grown up doing heavy labor under the hot sun. Maybe best of all, apple trees produce juicy, delicious apples. This is not necessarily a sexual innuendo. If the woman is talking about sex at all, she is much more restrained than other poets from the ancient world.[9] The fruit of the apple tree is simply an image of natural beauty that expresses her desire for a fruitful relationship. The man she is looking for not only protects but also provides.

Here is another comparison: the love of her beloved is like a banner—in this case, a banner that waves over the banqueting house where they will share dinner for two. This image comes from the army, where a banner is a military standard. Imagine the pennant of a medieval knight fluttering over his pavilion, or the flags that soldiers carried to the battlefield during the Civil War to identify their combat units. A banner is an image of power, authority, and identity. The woman is saying that her beloved's flag has captured her heart, not through any form of coercion, but by the strength of his character. Now she wants to be under the banner of his affection. If we wanted to find a contemporary analogy, it's like a girl wearing her boyfriend's football jersey as a token of affection and a public sign that they are together as a couple.

But what this young woman—this beautiful bride—wants to celebrate most of all is her beloved's affection. His banner over her is *love*. We get a picture of his affection in chapter 2, verse 6, where they are locked in a tender embrace. In verse 5 she is so lovesick—probably because her man is absent—that she needs to go lie down for a little while. But in verse 6 he is right there with her. His left hand is under her head, while his right arm is wrapped around her shoulder or perhaps her waist. If we could bring this couple into the twenty-first century, we would probably see them sitting close together on a couch and watching a movie.

At the risk of perpetuating gender stereotypes, we need to be faithful to the imagery of this passage. The lover in the Song of Songs is looking for security, and when she finds it, she celebrates it. Her example helps women know what to affirm in the men they love: both protection and affection. The Bible always strikes the perfect balance. Here it brings together strength and gentleness as manly qualities that deserve a woman's encouragement. For the woman to see this in him does not diminish her dignity. After all, he praises her in this Song as much as she praises him. When a lover and the beloved praise each other for different attributes, according to their unique design, with mutual respect and equal affection, their love for each other will grow.

Patience before Passion

Up until this point there has been a clear progression. Even without a conversation to define this relationship, we can tell that it is going somewhere. The Song of Songs started with a woman who wanted to be kissed, right on the lips. Apparently, this was before she had spent much time with the man she loved. But soon they started talking to each other, gazing into each other's eyes, embracing each other. . . . I think we can all see where this is going.

Yet the woman in the Song of Songs wants us to stop right there, before we take even one more step. At this point in the romance we get a warning so serious that she swears it with a solemn oath: "I adjure you, O daughters of Jerusalem, by the gazelles or the does of the field, that you not stir up or awaken love until it pleases" (Song 2:7; see also 3:5; 8:4).

This is not the way that people usually talk. But remember that this is a song, which is simply poetry set to music, and poetry uses imagery to communicate. The image here is of a gazelle, or a female deer. We get many comparisons like this in the Song of Songs. The writer expresses the beauty of the human body and protects the mystery of sex by speaking figuratively instead of literally. Deer and gazelles are beautiful animals. They are also fertile, so in the ancient world they were associated with lovemaking. Frankly, this young woman was thinking about sex.

Believe it or not, she was also thinking about God, who we should always keep in mind when we are talking about sex. We know that she was thinking about God because "the sounds of the Hebrew words for gazelles (*seba'ot*) and does of the field (*'ayelot hassadeh*) also deliberately recall the divine names *yhwh seba'ot* ('the Lord of Hosts') and *'el sadday* ('God Almighty')."[10] There is a double meaning in the biblical text—a sanctified double entendre. The beloved has something so important to say that she calls God as her witness.

Here the woman speaks to the "daughters of Jerusalem"—her bridesmaids, so to speak. These young single women are of marriageable age, and she wants to give them some good advice. So she says something like this: "Girlfriend, you do *not* want to get this hungry for a man until the time is right!" Sexual desire is like a sleeping lion: it is better left alone.

Somehow it seems significant that the person giving single people this advice is young and beautiful and about to experience her wedding night. Solomon gives similar advice to his son in the book of Proverbs, which is what you would expect a father to say. But the person speaking to us about sex in the Song of Songs is not someone so old you can hardly imagine her ever having sex; it's someone young and passionate and beautiful. She is not just saying no, either. She is saying yes, but she is saying yes only with the right person, and only at the right time. Sex is not something to rush into; neither is marriage. This is wisdom.

Sexual intimacy is one of the most powerful gifts that God ever created. Like most powerful gifts, it is also dangerous. We need to be careful with our sexuality, and this woman wants us to know that. True love really does wait. So she sings a love song about keeping our virginity, of all things, and about saving ourselves for marriage. She tells us "not to stir up or awaken love until it pleases."

When is the right time for sexual intimacy? The right time is when a man and a woman get married, of course. Marriage is the moral context for sex. It also happens to be the hermeneutical context for sex: the Bible interprets everything pertaining to sexual relations from the vantage point of marriage.

It would be hard to think of something more countercultural than telling people not to awaken their desires. Maybe this has always been the case. The Oxford professor and Christian apologist C. S. Lewis claimed that the Christian sexual ethic "is so difficult and so contrary to our instincts, that obviously either Christianity is wrong or our sexual instinct is wrong. One or the other."[11] Today we live in a culture that believes every desire should be satisfied. Therefore people constantly try to awaken our sexual interest. But every sexual image we see—every enticing advertisement and every pornographic picture—is a violation of the holy and difficult principle that sexual desire should not be stirred up at the wrong time.

The hookup culture on most college and university campuses today also runs counter to the biblical standard of divine wisdom. Too many young people go off to college with the expectation of sexual experimentation. In the words of Donna Freitas, who wrote *The End of Sex: How Hookup Culture Is Leaving a Generation Unhappy*, casual sex is "so ingrained in college life that if you're not doing it, then you're not getting the full college experience."[12]

Song of Songs 2 is one of those places where God tells us that he doesn't want us to have something that we want. God doesn't always do this, but he does it sometimes, and when he does, it always brings some degree of suffering. The suffering that comes from self-denial is a healthy part of daily life for every Christian. God does not say what he says because he wants to get in the way of our pleasure. Just the opposite! His wisdom is always for us, never against us. When it comes to our sexuality he doesn't want us to settle for smaller pleasures that surely will get in the way of greater satisfaction. This might include having a marriage that lasts, but more importantly, it definitely includes the deep joy of having a closer relationship with him, whether we are married or single. Sexual restraint is spiritually fruitful. One day the cross-bearing we do with our sexual desires will be crowned with honor and consummated in the eternal love of Jesus Christ.

The reason God tells us not to awaken sexual desire before its time is very simple: when we share sexual intimacy with the wrong person at the wrong time—or when we gratify sexual desire all by ourselves—we destroy relationships. Sex is like superglue: it is designed to form a lifetime bond between husband and wife. But when we use it in all the wrong ways, it loses its power. If we are not careful, the superglue of sex will end up losing its power to unite, like a sticky note that we have pressed down and pulled off a few dozen times. This is not to say that our sins cannot be forgiven, that our sexuality cannot be redeemed, or that the bonding power of sex cannot be restored in the context of a faithful marriage. But it does explain why even when your body and your culture say yes, the Holy Spirit may say, "Not now," "Not yet," or even "No, this is not the plan I have for you."

The gift of our sexuality is a huge test for us. God is calling all of us—in one way or another—to what one pastor has termed "consistent sexual sacrifice."[13] We all have a choice to make, whether we are married or single, and whether we desire the same sex or the opposite sex. Will we let our sinful desires govern our reading of Scripture, or will we let the Bible teach us what we should want? Will we let temptation take control, or will we honor God with our bodies by embracing his purposes for our sexuality?

A Passion for Purity

As we consider these questions, it is wise for us to consider carefully the example of Jesus. As a real man, with a real body, Jesus had the same sexual desires that any man has. Like us, he was called to preserve his purity by surrendering those desires to his Father's perfect will. In choosing chastity he denied himself the physical pleasure of sexual union, but he did not have to give up the gift of friendship or live anything less than a fulfilling life that counted for the kingdom.

What is really at stake in the sexual choices we make is our relationship to Jesus. Sex is never disconnected from the rest of spiritual life. In fact, it is as closely connected to our souls as anything else in the world. As Paul Tripp explains:

> Sex is presented in Scripture as a principal way a person expresses his submission to or rebellion against God. . . . Human beings live out of one of only two identities: that I am ultimate and autonomous or that I am created and dependent on God. Our sexuality constantly forces us to choose between these two identities. At the same time, our sin in this area shows us our need for God's mercy: It is when I am confronted with my utter inability to meet the demands of God's standards that I am also confronted with the reality and majesty of His grace. . . . Sex reveals my need of grace. God's call to sexual purity is as impossible for me to achieve without His help as it would have been for me to save myself.[14]

If we do not answer God's call to sexual purity, the gospel will not penetrate this area of our lives. But the more we pursue sexual purity, the more passion there will be in our relationship with Jesus. This is true for single people who offer celibacy as a gift to God—the gift of their sexuality. It is also true for married people who offer sexual fidelity as their gift to God. Our passion for Jesus will return whenever we choose to pursue purity—even if we have sinned repeatedly in the area of our sexuality. As soon as we move toward purity, we move toward Jesus. With this spiritual connection in mind, here is how Elisabeth Elliot posed the question we face in the choices we make about sex (or about anything else, for that matter): "When obedience to God contradicts what I think will give me pleasure, let me ask myself if I love Him."[15] Because if I do love Jesus, I will choose purity for him over pleasure for myself.

The Song of Songs is for lovers—not just in human relationships but also in our soul's relationship to God. Remember, the human experience of love and marriage always speaks to us about the deep mystery of redemption, in which God the Father promises to present us as a beautiful bride to his beloved Son. Thus the passion we see in the lover and the beloved from the Song of Songs—a passion they protect with their purity—calls us to fall deeper in love with Jesus Christ.

According to the imagery of the Song of Songs, Jesus is the apple tree of our salvation. He is the source of our rest and refreshment, whose fruit is sweet to our taste. He invites us to behold his rare beauty, even as he celebrates the beauty he has created in us. His banner over us is love—a banner that bears the emblem of the cross where he died for our sins (including all our sexual sins). Now he invites us into his banqueting house, where the bread and the wine on his table provide rich food for our souls.

The Savior who gives us this invitation knows what it means to surrender sexuality to the glory of God, for he lived with perfect purity. According to Hebrews 4:15, Jesus was as tempted to sexual sin as anyone. Yet he resisted. Forgoing the pleasures of sexual union was part of the loving obedience he offered to the Father. His crucified body was celibate. So is the glorious body of his resurrection triumph over sin and death.

What Jesus wants in return is our undivided affection. He wants all our love and all our selves, including the aspect of our bodies and souls that is sexual. This is why the people of God have turned to the Song of Songs again and again over the centuries. Our Beloved Savior is calling us into a deeper love. So we come to him with the prayer for affection and protection that Saint Augustine once prayed: "I cannot measure my love to know how much it falls short of being sufficient, but let my soul hasten to your embrace and never be turned away until it is hidden in the secret shelter of your presence."[16]

3

I'm for You, and You're for Me

The voice of my beloved!
    Behold, he comes,
leaping over the mountains,
    bounding over the hills.
My beloved is like a gazelle
    or a young stag.
Behold, there he stands
    behind our wall,
gazing through the windows,
    looking through the lattice.
My beloved speaks and says to me:
"Arise, my love, my beautiful one,
    and come away,
for behold, the winter is past;
    the rain is over and gone.
The flowers appear on the earth,
    the time of singing has come,
and the voice of the turtledove
    is heard in our land.
The fig tree ripens its figs,
    and the vines are in blossom;
    they give forth fragrance.

Arise, my love, my beautiful one,
  and come away.
O my dove, in the clefts of the rock,
  in the crannies of the cliff,
let me see your face,
  let me hear your voice,
for your voice is sweet,
  and your face is lovely.
Catch the foxes for us,
  the little foxes
that spoil the vineyards,
  for our vineyards are in blossom."

My beloved is mine, and I am his;
  he grazes among the lilies.
Until the day breathes
  and the shadows flee,
turn, my beloved, be like a gazelle
  or a young stag on cleft mountains.
On my bed by night
I sought him whom my soul loves;
  I sought him, but found him not.
I will rise now and go about the city,
  in the streets and in the squares;
I will seek him whom my soul loves.
  I sought him, but found him not.
The watchmen found me
  as they went about in the city.
"Have you seen him whom my soul loves?"
Scarcely had I passed them
  when I found him whom my soul loves.
I held him, and would not let him go
  until I had brought him into my mother's house,
  and into the chamber of her who conceived me.

I adjure you, O daughters of Jerusalem,
  by the gazelles or the does of the field,
that you not stir up or awaken love
  until it pleases. (Song 2:8–3:5)

Radio personality and baseball announcer Ernie Harwell called play-by-play for the Detroit Tigers for more than forty years. Two things distinguished his Hall of Fame career. First, he is the only announcer ever to be traded for a Major League Baseball player, catcher Cliff Dapper of the old Brooklyn Dodgers. Second, Harwell opened every season with a reading from sacred Scripture. He began his broadcast of the first Tiger game at Spring Training with these words from the Song of Solomon: "For, lo, the winter is past, the rain is over and gone; the flowers appear on the earth; the time of singing has come, and the voice of the turtledove is heard in our land" (Song 2:11–12 NKJV).

The original context for these eloquent words was not baseball, of course, but the smoldering romance between the man and the woman we meet in the Song of Songs. Springtime is for lovers, so the beloved groom used the sights and sounds of spring—warm sunshine, bright flowers, clear birdsongs—to invite his beautiful bride to come away and be his love. Through his words, the Holy Spirit hopes that we will hear our Savior's call to fall in love with him all over again and go away together to a place that is past all pain and sorrow.

Picture Perfect

Before we get into the details of this passage, we may find it helpful to remember the wider context. The Song of Songs is an album of love songs about a youthful romance that became a lifelong commitment. In all likelihood, these songs were matrimonial ballads—lyrics sung at weddings in ancient Israel to celebrate the gift of marriage. When we read them from beginning to end, they more or less tell us the story of a happy couple.

The songs do not show us this couple at their worst, for the most part, but usually at their best. If their relationship seems a little too perfect, this may be part of the point: the Holy Spirit is presenting "the perfect couple" so we know what love is supposed to look like. In this respect, the Song of Songs is like the box top for a jigsaw puzzle. When you dump the pieces on the table, they're a total mess; you need a picture to help put them into place. The Song of Songs is a picture of love for people who are still figuring out how the pieces fit together. It doesn't show us everything that's broken, but mainly shows us the way things were always meant to be.

Seeing the bigger picture is especially important because the Song of Songs is not just about human relationships; it is also about the soul's relationship to God. This does not mean that the book is a kind of code in which every detail stands for some spiritual reality. Strictly speaking, the Song of Songs is not an allegory. But marital love is one of the main ways that the Bible talks about God's desire for his people and about our eternal romance with Jesus Christ. We should never forget that we are betrothed to the Son of God and that as a result, everything the Bible says about the mystery of marriage is partly intended to help us fall more deeply in love with our Savior.

Understanding the Bible's romantic imagery, in which we are called "the bride of Christ," is a stretch for almost everyone. Roughly half of all Bible readers are men, who of course will never become brides. A fair number of us will always be single; in the providence of God, we will never be married. Some of us may not desire the opposite sex the way the lovers do in the Song of Songs. Nevertheless, every believer belongs to the bride of Christ. To say this another way, we are all engaged to be married to the Son of God. Although this analogy has its limits (as all analogies do), the Holy Spirit uses it to invite us into the pleasures of a closer relationship with our loving God. When we use our imagination and find ourselves in this love song, we are able to say to our Savior essentially what the woman says at the end of chapter 2: "My beloved is mine, and I am his" (v. 16).

Long-Distance Relationship

The last thing this beautiful young woman said to us was a warning that she will not hesitate to repeat, a warning not to be sexually active when it's not the right time to share sexual intimacy. But this does not mean that her desire has cooled. On the contrary, she is still hot for her beloved. She sees him in the distance, coming toward her, and then suddenly he shows up right on her doorstep:

> The voice of my beloved!
>   Behold, he comes,
> leaping over the mountains,
>   bounding over the hills.
> My beloved is like a gazelle
>   or a young stag.
> Behold, there he stands
>   behind our wall,
> gazing through the windows,
>   looking through the lattice. (2:8–9)

These verses are like a movie scene in which two lovers who have been far apart start running into one another's arms. Obviously, the woman is looking at her man with the eyes of affection. If he has any flaws, she doesn't notice them; she sees only how strong he is, how athletic and how good looking. He sounds a lot like Superman (leaping over all those tall mountains), but to her he was like a gazelle: graceful and beautiful.

There is a clear progression as this amazing man comes closer and closer. First the woman hears her beloved's voice; then she sees him running toward her; finally, as the camera moves in for a closeup, we see him right outside the door. Young men do have a way of hanging around the women they love. In this case, the young man is looking through the window to see if anyone's home. Rather than thinking of him as a creepy stalker, we should see him more like Romeo outside Juliet's window, hoping desperately that she will come out to the balcony, where he can see her.

In verses 10 to 13 their eyes meet, the harps and lyres softly begin to play, and they continue the flirtatious conversation that they began in the previous chapter:

> My beloved speaks and says to me:
> "Arise, my love, my beautiful one,
>   and come away,
> for behold, the winter is past;
>   the rain is over and gone.
> The flowers appear on the earth,
>   the time of singing has come,
> and the voice of the turtledove
>   is heard in our land.
> The fig tree ripens its figs,

and the vines are in blossom;
they give forth fragrance.
Arise, my love, my beautiful one,
and come away."

With these words, the beloved invokes the beauty of springtime as a compelling reason that this relationship should move toward marriage. In Illinois, where I live, the harbingers of spring are crocuses, daffodils, and the annual migration of warblers, as well as the final melt of snow. Springtime is like the dramatic scene in *The Lion, the Witch and the Wardrobe* when Aslan breaks the spell of winter and springtime comes to Narnia.[1] But in ancient Israel, as in many parts of the world, winter was the rainy season. So people looked forward to the time when the rains were over and gone, when flowers appeared in the desert, and turtledoves got busy making their nests.

As he pictures the scene, the beloved appeals to every sensation—sight, sound, and smell. In doing so, he is summoning all his poetic powers to win this woman's heart. He is also making a kind of argument. Back in verse 7 his lover warned him not to arouse love before its time. By celebrating the springtime—in all its fragrant, fruitful, melodic splendor—the beloved is trying to persuade her that the time for romance has finally come. If the figs are ripening on the tree and the turtledoves are making their nests, then it must be the season for love.

So the beloved invites the woman he loves to come away and be his love—an invitation he gives her twice in these verses: "Arise, my love, my beautiful one, and come away" (2:10, 13). Once again, the beloved celebrates his lover's beauty, only this time it sounds like a marriage proposal. What the man wants—more than anything else in the world—is to be with this woman all the time:

O my dove, in the clefts of the rock,
in the crannies of the cliff,
let me see your face,
let me hear your voice,
for your voice is sweet,
and your face is lovely. (2:14)

The dove is a lovebird, which presumably explains why "The Twelve Days of Christmas" talks about *two* turtledoves: they always come in pairs. The Song of Songs depicts one of these doves hiding in the mountains. This is an image of beauty but also of inaccessibility. Up until now, the woman has been out of reach, for she still belongs to her mother's household. Thus the man compares her to a turtledove nesting on the side of a cliff. The image reminds me of an amazing nest in the Grand Canyon of the Yellowstone, where ospreys meet on a towering pinnacle every year to make their home. The man in this song of all songs wants to get to a place where he can hear his lover's voice and see her face-to-face.

Before we hear how the woman responds to this invitation, we should pause to see the big picture of God's love. When the Bible says that God is our husband, and when it says that Jesus is the Bridegroom of our salvation, it means that we are loved with this kind of love—the ardent affection that we see in the Song of Songs. Sometimes we are tempted to think that somehow we are beneath God's notice or to imagine that we have done something so wrong (maybe something sexual) that God could never love us again, or to conclude on the basis of our present troubles that God is not for us but against us.

If this is what we think, then we need to hear—once again—the truth that establishes our identity and determines our destiny: we are loved with an everlasting love. Undying love led the

Son of God to leap past galaxies and bound through space to become a lowly human being on little planet Earth. Jesus came to win a lover's heart, whatever the cost. In the stirring words of one famous old hymn, "From heav'n he came and sought her, / to be his holy bride; / with his own blood he bought her, / and for her life he died."[2]

Costly love now compels our Savior to stand at the door and knock for entrance into our hearts. His love declares our true beauty and invites us to rise up from sin and even death so that we can go with him to our eternal home. What we read in the Song of Songs fundamentally is the same thing that God says to us in Jesus Christ: "Arise, my love, my beautiful one, and come away."

Protecting Love's Vineyard

The young woman's response to this loving invitation is surprising. Although she makes the strongest possible declaration of their commitment to each other, at the same time she sends her beloved away. She starts by saying something hard to understand:

> Catch the foxes for us,
>   the little foxes
> that spoil the vineyards,
>   for our vineyards are in blossom. (2:15)

Some scholars think that these words are spoken by the woman's brothers, who are giving their sister's suitor a personal and perhaps impossible challenge before they will permit him to marry their sister. He must become a fox catcher before he can become a bridegroom. Others speculate that this verse might be a familiar rhyme that workers used to sing in the vineyard when they were trying to protect their tender vines from ravenous animals.

Or perhaps the woman is drawing a subtle springtime analogy.[3] Earlier she described her body as a vineyard (1:6). If she is making the same comparison here, she is acknowledging that both she and her beloved are of marriageable age—their bodies are mature enough to become one flesh. Thus she is granting her beloved's argument that it is time for their love to blossom. But making it through puberty is hardly the only thing that matters in preparing for marriage. The woman knows that at this stage their relationship is as vulnerable as a juicy grape to a hungry fox. As their romance ripens, there is need for continued caution; this is the point of her analogy. Their love—and especially their sexuality—needs to be protected like a prized vineyard. It takes patience to cultivate the tender blossoms of a grapevine. Similarly, it takes patience to wait for a tender romance to become a love that lasts.

Getting ready for marriage also requires the assistance and oversight of people who know what they are doing. By using the plural form of the verb "to catch," the woman is asking the wider community of faith—the "fox catchers"—to help protect their purity. Every romantic relationship needs wise protection—from manipulation, from physical or emotional abuse, and from sexual transgression, with all of the spiritual damage that these mistakes can cause. Budding relationships also need to be safeguarded from the many attacks that Satan makes whenever God's sons and daughters imagine a future together that could make a difference in the world for his kingdom. Here the woman wisely pleads for their tender relationship to be protected from danger and destruction.

There are many ways to answer her appeal. Here is one of the most important: every Christian who is in a romantic relationship needs a mentor—specifically, a man or a woman (as the case may be) who knows what it means to be married in a way that gives honor and glory to God. A promising romance is too precious to squander and far too difficult for any couple to figure out on their own. It takes the wise counsel and faithful prayer support of the wider Christian community to catch "the little foxes" that spoil the vineyards of love and may prevent a romance from ever bearing abundant fruit. It seems clear, therefore, that anyone who is in a relationship that might lead to marriage should seek out mature spiritual guidance.

Notice carefully how the woman in the Song of Songs also takes personal responsibility for the passion and purity of her relationship with the man she loves. In verse 17 she says:

> Until the day breathes
>   and the shadows flee,
> turn, my beloved, be like a gazelle
>   or a young stag on cleft mountains.

The reference to "a young stag on cleft mountains" is not an invitation for her beloved to explore her anatomy; just the opposite. The verb "turn" means to "turn aside." Simply put, she is sending the young man away. She is telling him to go back where he came from at the beginning of this passage, when he was not at her house but on some faraway mountain. If we wonder why she does this, we probably get our answer in her repeated warning not to awaken love until its time. This bride-to-be wisely wants to wait for sexual passion until the arrival of her wedding day. Until then, she wants to make sure that clear boundaries for physical intimacy are put in place.

In the previous chapter we noted that the man in the Song of Songs is protective without ever being patronizing. Here we see that the woman in this love story is never passive but always proactive in pursuing what is best before God in their relationship. Here she takes responsibility for sexual purity. She should not have to do this alone, of course. God holds men fully responsible for what they do with their bodies and for how they treat women (especially if they are stronger physically, as they often are). But in this passage we see a godly woman exercise appropriate caution. Since it is not yet time for sexual intimacy, she turns him away until their wedding day.

Young people often ask where "the line" is. They want to know how far they can go before breaking God's law for physical or sexual intimacy. This is the wrong question to ask, of course. A better question is, "How can I protect the purity of the person I say that I love?" But if a guideline is needed, here is a simple one to follow: two people who are not married should not touch the sexual parts of one another's bodies.

The woman in the Song of Songs is not saying *no* or *never* to her beloved; she's saying *not yet*. She says this in a way that strengthens their relationship. Verse 16 begins with one of the most beautiful phrases in the Bible: "My beloved is mine, and I am his." Then the verse ends with a kiss. Later in the Song of Songs, the woman will compare her beloved's lips to a bed of lilies (5:13). Similarly, when she says here that "he grazes among the lilies," she is kissing his lily lips (which might not be the way that we ordinarily would talk, but we always have to make allowances for people in love).

This couple belongs together, and because they belong together, they belong to one another. Earlier the woman triumphantly placed herself under the banner of her beloved's affection (2:4). But we should not think for a moment that she belongs to him without him also belonging to her. In the mutuality of their romance, they both possess and are possessed by the affection of the one they love. Presumably at this stage of their love story they are engaged to be married. Although they have not yet taken the vows of holy matrimony, they are promised to one another. This is the context for the lovers' bold declaration of mutual possession.

The Man of Her Dreams

With the final verses of chapter 2 we come to the close of day. As badly as these two lovers want each other, and as much as they are committed to one another, they kiss each other good night and then wisely go their separate ways.

It is agony for them to be apart. Separation is one of the trials of being truly in love but not yet properly married. It's hard to wait for the honeymoon! Thus it is not surprising that the woman spends the rest of the night dreaming about the man of her dreams, as chapter 3 opens with what appears to be a dream sequence. Observing how the narrative "moves between the world of dream and wakefulness," Pico Iyer notes that "a beloved is never so present to us, never felt and remembered with such vividness and intensity as when he or she is gone from us."[4] This phenomenon explains why, when the woman awoke, she remembered her dream with such perfect clarity:

> On my bed by night
> I sought him whom my soul loves;
>   I sought him, but found him not.
> I will rise now and go about the city,
>   in the streets and in the squares;

I will seek him whom my soul loves.
    I sought him, but found him not.
The watchmen found me
    as they went about the city.
"Have you seen him whom my soul loves?" (3:1–3)

If the grammatical form of the Hebrew verb "I sought" is any indication, the same thing happened night after night: the woman in the Song of Songs had a recurring dream in which she looked everywhere for the man she loved, until finally she found him. Dreams usually focus on either our hopes or our fears, and this dream was about both. As soon as the woman sent her beloved away—the man she hoped to marry—suddenly she was afraid that she would never see him again.

So the woman in love left the safety of her home to go out and look for her fiancé. When she couldn't find him, she didn't give up but kept looking. When it came to the love in this relationship, she wasn't just on the receiving end; she was willing to pursue love and even fight for it. Ready to face any danger, she went out into the city streets late at night desperate to find her lover. She looked everywhere and asked everyone. He was nowhere to be found! But then, just as suddenly as she had lost him, she found him again:

Scarcely had I passed them
    when I found him whom my soul loves.
I held him, and would not let him go
    until I had brought him into my mother's house,
    and into the chamber of her who conceived me. (3:4)

Once she relocated him, she did what any young woman would do when she found the man of her dreams: she took him straight home to meet her mother. By referring to her mother's bedchamber, the woman is hinting—not too subtly—that she wants to get married and start a family. Here the Bible affirms one of God's primary purposes for marriage: to produce godly offspring. This does not mean that every couple will receive the gift of children; in the providence of God, some couples remain childless. But this love story does remind us that every Christian couple should be open to the high calling of parenthood.

Not incidentally, then, the woman in the Song of Songs also wants to share sexual intimacy with her beloved. What else are bedchambers for? The Bible does nothing to diminish this natural desire in a woman but positively celebrates it, provided that sex is shared in its proper context.

Even in her dreams, the young woman in Solomon's song is going about all of this in the right way. She wants to receive her family's blessing. Her positive example shows us one good way to test whether we are in the right romantic relationship: if we are, then we will not hide it from the people who know us the best and care about us the most, but we will invite them to participate in what is happening in our lives. A healthy romance is never private. One of the reasons this story has such a happy ending is that this couple brings their desire for lasting intimacy under the care of their community, with the blessing of their family. Not every couple receives the benefit of a family blessing. On rare occasions, when parents withhold their favor for reasons that do not honor God, a Christian couple may need to proceed with their wedding plans. But the biblical ideal is for couples to ask for and receive the full blessing of their families.

A Repeated Warning

The woman in this love song must have been a big sister, because even in her moments of greatest happiness, when she sees her dreams coming to life, she finds it necessary to give the same warning that she gave before:

> I adjure you, O daughters of Jerusalem,
> by the gazelles or the does of the field,
> that you not stir up or awaken love
> until it pleases. (3:5; cf. 2:7)

The woman is not just talking about love in this verse; she's talking about sex. She is telling us once again that true love waits. She says this not to deny our sexual desires, but to teach us to dedicate our sexuality to God. Practicing celibacy is not simply refraining from sex; it is an active and positive way of offering ourselves to God. Nor is the woman who speaks trying to stigmatize sexual sin, as if one kind of sin is more sinful than another. Her purpose rather is to help us avoid making the mistakes that break lovers' hearts and sometimes ruin people's lives.

God has mercy for people who fail to heed this warning. Of course he does! God always has mercy. As we saw when we started the Song of Songs and looked at the overall love story that the Bible tells, Jesus Christ is busy purifying everything unholy in us so that we might become his virgin bride. Not only did Jesus protect the vineyard of his own body by resisting the temptation to sexual sin, but he also restored our own spoiled vineyards through his death on the cross. Therefore, God's promise of forgiveness is as true for our sexual transgressions as it is for anything: "If we confess our sins, he is faithful and just to forgive us our sins and to cleanse us from all unrighteousness" (1 John 1:9). By his grace, God has made peace with us, even after all our spiritual promiscuity. We should never forget this, especially if we still feel guilty sometimes about sins that we have already confessed. Our iniquity is not our identity. Our sexual or marital history may be marred by failure. This is true for most people, to one degree or another. But our history is not our destiny. What counts far more than our record of wrongs is the perfect faithfulness of our heavenly husband. We are holy in Jesus.

We also need to be careful not to think that sexual sins are worse than other sins, or that they carry a special stigma. C. S. Lewis corrects this misperception in *Mere Christianity*, where he writes:

> Though I have had to speak at some length about sex, I want to make it as clear as I possibly can that the centre of Christian morality is not here. If anyone thinks that Christians regard unchastity as the supreme vice, he is quite wrong. The sins of the flesh are bad, but they are the least bad of all sins. All the worst pleasures are purely spiritual: the pleasure of putting other people in the wrong, of bossing and patronizing and spoiling sport, and backbiting; the pleasure of power, of hatred. . . . That is why a cold, self-righteous prig who goes regularly to church may be far nearer to hell than a prostitute. But, of course, it is better to be neither.[5]

Having made these qualifications, we shouldn't miss the Bible's warnings either. What the Bible says about sexual sin was written to help us. God loves us and wants the best for us. He knows that even when sin is forgiven, it can still have negative consequences. So the Song of Songs says again what it said before: do not say anything, look at anything, or touch anything to arouse sexual desire until the time is right. This is wise counsel in every situation and at every stage of life. It is wise for young people and old people, wise for married people and single people, wise for those who are attracted to the same sex or the opposite sex. It is wise for anyone and everyone.

One of the main reasons the Bible tells us not to arouse desire unwisely is that the Holy Spirit does not want anything to get in the way of our soul's relationship with our Savior. God wants everything for us that the lovers had in the Song of Songs, and more. He wants to be the Redeemer of our dreams. He wants us to want to be with him all the time. He wants us to seek him and find him and never let him go. He wants us to be able to say, "My beloved is mine, and I am his." But it is hard for any of this to happen the way it should if we insist on taking sex for ourselves instead of giving it over to God and protecting it in the safe home of covenant matrimony.

What kind of relationship do you want to have with God? Look for the kind of affection that the French Carmelite Thérèse of Lisieux expressed when she received her first Communion. Thérèse testified: "It was a kiss of love; I knew that I was loved and I declared, 'I love You and I give myself to You forever!'"[6] This is the heart of love that the Holy Spirit wants to give us. It is also the heart that Jesus is looking for when he says, "Arise, my love, my beautiful one, and come away."

4

Royal Wedding

What is that coming up from the wilderness
    like columns of smoke,
perfumed with myrrh and frankincense,
    with all the fragrant powders of a merchant?
Behold, it is the litter of Solomon!
Around it are sixty mighty men,
    some of the mighty men of Israel,
all of them wearing swords
    and expert in war,
each with his sword at his thigh,
    against terror by night.
King Solomon made himself a carriage
    from the wood of Lebanon.
He made its posts of silver,
    its back of gold, its seat of purple;
its interior was inlaid with love
    by the daughters of Jerusalem.
Go out, O daughters of Zion,
    and look upon King Solomon,
with the crown with which his mother crowned him
    on the day of his wedding,
    on the day of the gladness of his heart.

Behold, you are beautiful, my love,
    behold, you are beautiful!
Your eyes are doves
    behind your veil.
Your hair is like a flock of goats
    leaping down the slopes of Gilead.
Your teeth are like a flock of shorn ewes
    that have come up from the washing,
all of which bear twins,
    and not one among them has lost its young.
Your lips are like a scarlet thread,
    and your mouth is lovely.
Your cheeks are like halves of a pomegranate
    behind your veil.
Your neck is like the tower of David,
    built in rows of stone;
on it hang a thousand shields,
    all of them shields of warriors.
Your two breasts are like two fawns,
    twins of a gazelle,
    that graze among the lilies.

Until the day breathes
    and the shadows flee,
I will go away to the mountain of myrrh
    and the hill of frankincense.
You are altogether beautiful, my love;
    there is no flaw in you.
Come with me from Lebanon, my bride;
    come with me from Lebanon.
Depart from the peak of Amana,
    from the peak of Senir and Hermon,
from the dens of lions,
    from the mountains of leopards.

You have captivated my heart, my sister, my bride;
you have captivated my heart with one glance of your eyes,
with one jewel of your necklace.
How beautiful is your love, my sister, my bride!
How much better is your love than wine,
and the fragrance of your oils than any spice!
Your lips drip nectar, my bride;
honey and milk are under your tongue;
the fragrance of your garments is like the fragrance of Lebanon.
A garden locked is my sister, my bride,
a spring locked, a fountain sealed.
Your shoots are an orchard of pomegranates
with all choicest fruits,
henna with nard,
nard and saffron, calamus and cinnamon,
with all trees of frankincense,
myrrh and aloes,
with all choice spices—
a garden fountain, a well of living water,
and flowing streams from Lebanon.

Awake, O north wind,
and come, O south wind!
Blow upon my garden,
let its spices flow.

Let my beloved come to his garden,
and eat its choicest fruits.

I came to my garden, my sister, my bride,
I gathered my myrrh with my spice,
I ate my honeycomb with my honey,
I drank my wine with my milk.

Eat, friends, drink,
and be drunk with love! (3:6–5:1)

As a pastor, I have had the privilege of performing many weddings. One of the most remarkable of these ceremonies was the exchange of vows between the late Dr. C. Everett Koop and my friend Cora Hogue. Dr. Koop famously served as United States surgeon general during the Reagan Administration, and Ms. Hogue was a friend and colleague in ministry from Philadelphia's Tenth Presbyterian Church.

Dr. Koop was in his nineties when I performed their wedding (this was his second marriage, after his first wife died of cancer). With his full white beard, Dr. Koop was a very distinguished-looking man—especially when he wore his surgeon general's uniform covered with medals and other official decorations. His beloved Cora looked equally distinguished, with her silver hair and radiant wedding gown.

After the happy couple had exchanged their vows, they lingered to greet their guests. Since there were five hundred or so in attendance, the newlyweds chose to sit rather than to stand. Two large, high-backed chairs were brought out and set at the front of the sanctuary, almost like two thrones. Afterward, I spoke with an international student from Japan. This was her first American wedding, and what impressed her most was the splendor of the bride and the groom. "They look like the king and the queen," she said.

We could say something similar about the happy couple that gets married in the Song of Songs, whose wedding is described with reference to King Solomon and his court. Some scholars take this literally and see Solomon as the bridegroom. Others say that the author uses the famous king to set up a contrast. Solomon's proud finery (to say nothing of his foolish adultery—remember how many wives he had) stands in sharp contrast to the simple beauty and humble purity of the countryside couple who exchange their wedding vows in the Song of Songs.

My own interpretation differs from both of these scholarly viewpoints. I think the Song of Songs sets a simple wedding in the context of the royal court in order to elevate marriage and display its true grandeur. The author is drawing a positive comparison between Solomon and the couple he sings about. This makes good sense, because every godly wedding is a royal wedding. Since God is a great king, whenever one of his sons marries one of his daughters, it is the marriage of a prince and princess.

Solomon's Approach

In chapters 3 and 4 we finally get to the wedding day—and also the wedding night! As a reminder, the Song of Songs is a collection of love songs that loosely tell the story of an intense romance becoming a lifelong covenant.

Typically these songs would have been sung during the weeklong celebration of an Israelite wedding. Chapter 1 began with a woman expressing her passionate desire for the man of her dreams. He wanted her just as badly as she wanted him, but they both wanted the blessing that would come only with pursuing the right relationship in the right way at the right time. So they sought the counsel of godly people in their community, who cautioned them to observe proper sexual boundaries.

At times it was frustrating for the two young lovers to stay pure. In fact, it may have seemed like a kind of suffering, for chastity is a sacred sacrifice to God. Yet their relationship kept moving closer and closer. In chapter 2 the man declared that it was springtime, the season for making love. The woman righteously reminded him that they were not ready to consummate their relationship. Still, she wanted to know him better, so she brought her beloved home for the blessing that only her family could give.

All of this forms the context for the fragrant question that someone asks in the following chapter:

> What is that coming up from the wilderness
> like columns of smoke,
> perfumed with myrrh and frankincense,
> with all the fragrant powders of a merchant? (3:6)

The verses that follow provide one answer. What is coming up from the wilderness? Why, it is a royal wedding procession:

> Behold, it is the litter of Solomon!
> Around it are sixty mighty men,
> some of the mighty men of Israel,
> all of them wearing swords
> and expert in war,
> each with his sword at his thigh,
> against terror by night.
> King Solomon made himself a carriage
> from the wood of Lebanon.
> He made its posts of silver,
> its back of gold, its seat of purple;
> its interior was inlaid with love
> by the daughters of Jersualem.

> Go out, O daughters of Zion,
> and look upon King Solomon,
> with the crown with which his mother crowned him
> on the day of his wedding,
> on the day of the gladness of his heart. (3:7–11)

If we know the facts of Solomon's life, it is easy to find a lot of problems in these verses. Why did the king need sixty bodyguards in order to feel safe in his bed at night? Presumably because he was afraid of getting assassinated. His bed sounds magnificent. With its silver posts, golden headboard, wooden inlay, and purple quilts it must have caught people's attention as it was being carried up to Jerusalem. Think of the millions of Americans who woke up early to watch the royal wedding of Prince William to Kate Middleton; they wanted to catch every detail, live from London. Yet we know that Solomon had seven hundred wives and three hundred concubines, and it's hard not to think about the king's appalling promiscuity when we read that his bed was "inlaid with love" (3:10).

None of this seems to trouble the author of the Song of Songs, however. The mood of these verses is entirely positive. The singer is celebrating the king, not criticizing him or regarding him with cynicism. This leads me to believe that the Song of Songs is showing us Solomon as he should have been, in all his royal majesty. The dignity of the kingly bridegroom is meant to heighten our expectancy. This will be a wedding fit for a king.

Here Comes the Bride!

At the beginning of chapter 4 the beloved does what every bridegroom should do: he shifts our attention to the bride. This happens in every wedding. Until the bride walks in, everyone looks at the groom. But as soon as she walks down the aisle, all eyes are on her.

To celebrate the beauty of his beloved bride, the groom sings what literature scholars call an "epithalamion"—in other words, a wedding song. Right at the center of the Song of Songs, in a passage running in chapter 4 from verse 1 to verse 15, he sets the beauty of his bride to music.

These verses give us a second answer to the question that was asked in the middle of chapter 3: "What is that coming up from the wilderness?" (v. 6). The first answer was Solomon's wedding procession. But the question is really *who*, not *what*, and in Hebrew the form of the interrogative demands a feminine answer (cf. 6:10 and 8:5). So to ask the question again, more accurately, "Who is this coming up from the wilderness?" In chapter 4 the answer is a bride beautifully adorned for her husband—the country girl who first captivated us in the opening verses of the Song of Songs. She is the one who is "perfumed with myrrh and frankincense, with all the fragrant powders of a merchant" (3:6; cf. 4:6). Not even Solomon in all his splendor could compare with her rare beauty.

As the groom celebrates his bride, he starts carrying her toward the wedding chamber. He says, "Behold, you are beautiful, my love." Then he says it again: "behold, you are beautiful!" (4:1). As he feasts his eyes on her beauty, he describes some of her best features, in a literary form known as an "emblematic blazon." In other words, he offers a poem "that praises, by listing, the beautiful features or virtuous qualities of the beloved."[1] The groom has done this before, but this time he goes into more detail. This is appropriate, because we are rapidly approaching the moment that this couple has been longing for: their wedding night. Think of chapter 4 as the verbal foreplay that precedes the consummation of their wedding vows.

As the groom runs his eyes over his lover's body, he starts with her eyes, which is where he started in chapter 1, at the window to her soul. "Your eyes are doves," he says, "behind your veil" (another wedding image). Her hair "is like a flock of goats leaping down the slopes of Gilead" (4:1); in other words, her tresses are long and flowing. Then the groom describes her teeth, and again he uses imagery familiar from the countryside that his bride knew and loved: "Your teeth are like a flock of shorn ewes that have come up from the washing, all of which bear twins, and not one among them has lost its young" (4:2). This is not the way people usually talk today, but it is not hard to see the points of comparison. His bride has perfect teeth. They are as white as a flock of sheep at shearing time. None of them are missing, which may seem like a small thing to us, but remember that in those days not even Solomon could find a good orthodontist.

Next the beloved talks about the rest of his lover's face: "Your lips are like a scarlet thread, and your mouth is lovely. Your cheeks are like halves of a pomegranate behind your veil" (4:3). The modesty of her wedding veil cannot conceal the beauty of her face; her rosy cheeks remind her husband of ripe fruit.

Then the groom lowers his gaze a little: "Your neck is like the tower of David, built in rows of stone; on it hang a thousand shields, all of them shields of warriors" (4:4). The bride stands tall. Evidently she is adorned with rows of necklaces that remind the groom of the glittering shields on the walls of David's fortress. Next he looks at her breasts. How does he describe them? They "are like two fawns, twins of a gazelle"

(4:5; cf. Prov. 5:19). Once again, the singer uses marvelous imagery drawn from the world of nature. The fawn is a picture of gentleness and fertility. Fawns often come in pairs, like two breasts, and all we usually catch is a glimpse of them as they slip into the woods. Under the inspiration of the Holy Spirit, this love poetry is erotic without degenerating into something pornographic.

That is all the farther the groom goes, at least for now. And it's all the farther he needs to go. He has described seven parts of his beloved's anatomy: her eyes, hair, teeth, lips, cheeks, neck, and breasts. Since seven is the biblical number of completion and perfection, he has said all that needs to be said. The dazzled groom sums it all up in verse 7: "You are altogether beautiful, my love; there is no flaw in you."

In the Garden of Delight

What the groom wants to do now, of course, is take this woman to bed and make love to her all night long. The invitation he gives her is poetical, not literal, but his meaning is clear enough. "Until the day breathes and the shadows flee," he says, "I will go away to the mountain of myrrh and the hill of frankincense. . . . Come with me from Lebanon, my bride; come with me from Lebanon. Depart from the peak of Amana, from the peak of Senir and Hermon, from the dens of lions, from the mountains of leopards" (4:6, 8).[2]

The context for this lovemaking makes all the difference. Here, at the center of the Song of Songs, where a loving relationship is consummated through sexual intimacy, the lover repeatedly refers to his beloved as his "bride." This word appears in verses 8, 9, 10, 11, and 12, and then again at the beginning of chapter 5, demonstrating beyond all doubt that the Song of

Songs is a wedding song. This terminology places everything that the book says about sex securely within the boundaries of the only divinely approved partnership for sexual relations, namely, marriage.

It is only within the bonds of covenant matrimony that it is appropriate for this man to use the first-person-singular possessive pronoun as often as he does. He says "my" twenty times in this passage (!), including verse 9, where he says, "my bride." Similarly, it is only in the context of wedding vows that it is appropriate for him to compare her body to the Promised Land: "Your lips drip nectar . . . , honey and milk are under your tongue; the fragrance of your garments is like the fragrance of Lebanon" (4:11). The groom is not just saying that his bride is "sugar and spice, and everything nice." By using the language of milk and honey, he is comparing her to the land that God promised his people to possess—a land that the Bible often describes as "flowing with milk and honey." Now that the lover and beloved have become man and wife, they belong to one another.

This is not the way that single people should ever act or think, as if someone else's body belonged to them. But within the bond of covenant matrimony, the Bible teaches that "the wife does not have authority over her own body, but the husband does. Likewise the husband does not have authority over his own body, but the wife does" (1 Cor. 7:4). With this biblical perspective in mind, Doug O'Donnell defines sexual intercourse as "an inexplicable act of mutual possession, passion, and submission: I give my total self to you, and you give your total self to me."[3] Marriage is the only place where a man and a woman belong to one another sexually, which is not a license for abuse but an invitation to paradise.

Up until now, these two lovers have protected their purity. Rather than exploiting each other or experimenting with each other, as people often do in our permissive society, they had safeguarded their sexuality. This helps to explain why the groom compares his bride to a private garden:

> A garden locked is my sister, my bride,
>   a spring locked, a fountain sealed.
> Your shoots are an orchard of pomegranates
>   with all choicest fruits,
>   henna with nard,
> nard and saffron, calamus and cinnamon,
>   with all trees of frankincense,
> myrrh and aloes,
>   with all choice spices—
> a garden fountain, a well of living water,
>   and flowing streams from Lebanon. (4:12–15)

Generally speaking, there were no public parks in the ancient world. The only gardens were places of privilege that were kept under lock and key. Here the bridegroom describes one such paradise, filled with every fruit and spice that gets mentioned elsewhere in the Song of Songs.[4] Until now, the fruits of physical intimacy have been off-limits. But listen to the invitation that the bride gives her beloved groom on their wedding night. Before they were married, she had often spoken a cautionary word, warning her sisters not to awaken love before its time. But now she gives her full consent. Indeed, she initiates sexual intimacy by inviting her beloved to claim her body as a garden of delight:

> Awake, O north wind,
>   and come, O south wind!

Blow upon my garden,
  let its spices flow.
Let my beloved come to his garden,
  and eat its choicest fruits. (4:16)

The groom does not hesitate but enters the unlocked garden of sexual pleasure:

I came to my garden, my sister, my bride.
  I gathered my myrrh with my spice,
  I ate my honeycomb with my honey,
  I drank my wine with my milk. (5:1)

More than this the happy couple will not say, which is part of what makes the Song of Songs suitable for audiences of all ages. In these two verses, which form the exact center of the Song of Songs—the climax, so to speak, with 111 lines before and 111 lines after[5]—the Bible brings us to the threshold of the bridal suite. Unlike our own culture, which usually brings sex way too far out into the open, the Song of Songs takes us right to the edge. We get close enough to sense the breathtaking beauty of sexual love in covenant marriage. Then the groom gently shuts the door, and his bride pulls down the shade, while we stand outside with the rest of their bridal party and join their friends and family in pronouncing the benediction of the covenant community: "Eat, friends, drink, and be drunk with love!" (5:1).

The Sex of Joy

What we see in the middle of the Song of Songs is the pleasure of sex the way God designed its goodness all the way back at the beginning, in the garden of Eden. There is nothing sinful here—nothing tawdry, vulgar, selfish, manipulative, or abusive. It is all beautiful and pure and innocent, and therefore it brings true joy to the happy couple and greater glory to God. The joy of the happy biblical couple reminds me of the time I explained sexual relations to one of my children, and he burst into a huge grin of unadulterated happiness in the purposes of God. "Really?!?" he said. There is joy—not only pleasure, but joy—in sex the way that God meant it to be.

Part of what makes this joy possible is that the Song is not just about sex; it is also about love. Nor is it only about bodies; it is about whole persons. We see this in the familial term that the groom typically pairs with the word "bride." He calls his lover not only his "bride" but also his "sister." This term of endearment connotes the kind of intimacy that we often see in a brother and sister who are close in age and understand each other better than anyone else in the world—even better than their own parents. The relationship at the center of the Song of Songs is not a sexual hookup; it is a spiritual friendship, and this is essential to their joy.

We see the depth of the couple's friendship in the declaration that the groom makes in chapter 4, verse 9: "You have captivated my heart, my sister, my bride; you have captivated my heart with one glance of your eyes, with one jewel of your necklace." It sounds like love at first sight. But perhaps more significant is what the man is sharing about himself. Up until this point, he has spent most of his time talking about the woman he loves, especially her appearance. But here he opens up his heart, which in the biblical world means more than simply his feelings or emotions. When he says that she has captivated his heart, he means that he loves her with his whole person: mind, heart, and soul, as well as body. And what he loves is *her* whole person: his sister-bride is "altogether beautiful" to him (4:7).

Through the Song of Songs, God is showing us sex and also marriage the way that he originally intended, as the spiritual union of two different people who become one flesh. The Holy Spirit wants us to see the marriage relationship in all of its divinely designed beauty, including the physical beauty of sexual love. C. S. Lewis said he knew that

> some muddle-headed Christians have talked as if Christianity thought that sex, or the body . . . were bad in themselves. But they were wrong. Christianity is almost the only one of the great religions which thoroughly approves of the body—which believes that matter is good, that God Himself once took on a human body, that some kind of body is going to be given to us even in Heaven and is going to be an essential part of our happiness.[6]

There is nothing bad about sex the way that God made it; it's all good—so good that in this passage it seems almost perfect.

The Song of Songs gives us a picture of the perfect marriage so that we know what it looks like and can live in that direction. Some of us get married, and it is crucially important for us to know that sex is for joy, and marriage is for spiritual friendship. But not all of us are called to be married. Whether this is our preference, or not, some of us are called to be single—"for the sake of the kingdom of heaven," as Jesus put it (Matt. 19:12). Furthermore, most people who do get married are single for a significant part of their lives, either before they get married or afterward. So what does this passage say to people who aren't married now and maybe never will be?

It says at least two things. One is that the sacrifice we make in pursuing sexual purity is a precious gift to God. Practicing celibacy is not merely refraining from any form of sexual intimacy; it is the active choice to dedicate our bodies to God. By seeking holiness (however imperfectly, for we all stumble in various ways) we take the sacred gift of our sexuality and lay it on God's altar. The more we see how beautiful sex is—especially in the Song of Songs—the more we understand how precious the gift of our sexuality is. Perhaps this helps to explain why men and women who surrender sex to the purposes of God have such life-giving influence. The lives of single men like theologian John Stott and single women like missionary Helen Roseveare display the supreme value of the kingdom of Jesus Christ over all earthly pleasures.

We remember too rarely that of all the major monotheistic religions, "only Christianity affirms singleness as a distinctive calling and gift within the community of God's people."[7] Christianity does this because the Bible does it. Single people are not second-class in the story of salvation. The clearest proof of this is Jesus himself, who led a loving and perfectly fulfilling human life without ever getting married or sharing sexual intimacy with anyone. We do not need to get married or experience sexual pleasure in order for God's plan for us to be good, or for us to have a satisfying life. Single people, as well as married people, find their fulfillment in the love story that includes everyone in the Christian community. Barry Danylak writes about this in his marvelous little book *A Biblical Theology of Singleness*:

> Though it may be a life without the joys of having a spouse and physical offspring, the New Testament nevertheless affirms singleness as a calling within the church. The place and contribution of singleness arises naturally out of the biblical storyline as God's redemptive hope unfolds to all

> humanity through Christ. In Christ a new community is being built, a community of male and female, Jew and Gentile, rich and poor, married and single. Singleness reflects important aspects of this community in a distinctive way. In affirming singleness as a calling and a gift, the New Testament also offers a message of hope and inclusion for those who are single.[8]

Remember as well that the Song of Songs is not only or even primarily about sex; it is more about love. It is not merely about love for another person, either: at its deepest level, the Song of Songs is about the soul's love relationship with the living God. Sexuality and spirituality are deeply related. Here is how Dan Allender and Tremper Longman describe their connection: "God gave us sex to arouse and satisfy a hunger for intimacy. Sexuality arouses a desire for union. Sexual consummation satisfies the desire, but it also mysteriously creates a hunger for more—not only for more sex, but also for a taste of ultimate union, the final reconciliation with God."[9]

Only God can satisfy our hunger for intimacy. The Bible gives us the picture of a perfect marriage to awaken our sense of longing for him. This is true for all of us, whether we are married or single. As believers in Christ we are destined to become a beautiful bride—the kind of bride described in Song of Songs 4, who is so totally beautiful that she doesn't even have one tiny flaw. She is like the radiant bride described in Ephesians 5, who is "holy and without blemish," "without spot or wrinkle or any such thing" (v. 27). Nothing in our present experience lives up to this kind of perfection. We live with a certain amount of dissatisfaction all the time. We are often disappointed and sometimes disheartened, even in the best friendship or happiest marriage.

The Bible is completely honest about life as it really is; most of the time it shows us the world in all its brokenness and people in all their sin.

But there are also passages like this one, where the Bible shows us the way things were meant to be. The Word of God is not being unrealistic when it does this; instead, it is holding out a promise. We desperately want everything to be right with the world. This in itself is a clue that we were made for eternity. In fact, it is more than a hint: it's an invitation. Through the Song of Songs, Jesus is calling us to come away and be his love. "There is a God above," writes Ray Ortlund Jr., "with love in his eyes for us and infinite joy to offer us, and he has set himself upon winning our hearts for himself alone."[10] Some day—on the happy day when the Father gives a bride to his Son—we will become the beauty that we have always longed for. We will also share the friendship with Jesus that we have always wanted. By the gift of God's grace, we will enter into the never-ending love of a match made in heaven.

A wedding dress from World War II beautifully illustrates our joyful destiny. Toward the end of the war, Major Claude Hensinger jumped from the cockpit of his flaming B-29 bomber and safely floated to the ground. After landing, he used his parachute as a pillow and blanket to keep warm while he waited to be rescued. Hensinger made it back home safely, and when he proposed to his girlfriend, Ruth, a few years later, he offered his life-saving parachute as the fabric to create her wedding gown. A local seamstress used the silky material to create a stunning work of art that is now preserved at the Smithsonian's National Museum of American History in Washington, DC.[11]

This is more or less our story too. First Jesus rescues us from the flames of judgment by his death on the cross. Then he asks us to be married to him forever. And when it comes time for us to celebrate our union, he provides a beautiful white wedding dress that is made from the perfect cloth of his salvation.

5

Lovers' Quarrel

I slept, but my heart was awake.
A sound! My beloved is knocking.
"Open to me, my sister, my love,
    my dove, my perfect one,
for my head is wet with dew,
    my locks with the drops of the night."
I had put off my garment;
    how could I put it on?
I had bathed my feet;
    how could I soil them?
My beloved put his hand to the latch,
    and my heart was thrilled within me.
I arose to open to my beloved,
    and my hands dripped with myrrh,
my fingers with liquid myrrh,
    on the handles of the bolt.
I opened to my beloved,
    but my beloved had turned and gone.
My soul failed me when he spoke.
I sought him, but found him not;
    I called him, but he gave no answer.
The watchmen found me
    as they went about in the city;

they beat me, they bruised me,
    they took away my veil,
    those watchmen of the walls.
I adjure you, O daughters of Jerusalem,
    if you find my beloved,
that you tell him
    I am sick with love.

What is your beloved more than another beloved,
    O most beautiful among women?
What is your beloved more than another beloved,
    that you thus adjure us?

My beloved is radiant and ruddy,
    distinguished among ten thousand.
His head is the finest gold;
    his locks are wavy,
    black as a raven.
His eyes are like doves
    beside streams of water,
bathed in milk,
    sitting beside a full pool.
His cheeks are like beds of spices,
    mounds of sweet-smelling herbs.
His lips are lilies,
    dripping liquid myrrh.
His arms are rods of gold,
    set with jewels.
His body is polished ivory,
    bedecked with sapphires.
His legs are alabaster columns,
    set on bases of gold.
His appearance is like Lebanon,
    choice as the cedars.

His mouth is most sweet,
  and he is altogether desirable.
This is my beloved and this is my friend,
  O daughters of Jerusalem.

Where has your beloved gone,
  O most beautiful among women?
Where has your beloved turned,
  that we may seek him with you?

My beloved has gone down to his garden
  to the beds of spices,
to graze in the gardens
  and to gather lilies.
I am my beloved's and my beloved is mine;
  he grazes among the lilies. (5:2–6:3)

It is sad but true: my wife Lisa and I had a huge fight on our honeymoon—on the second day or maybe the third. She might remember what we fought about, but I don't. I almost never do, which serves as a good reminder that most of the things we fight about are not nearly as important as they seem to be at the time. Another thing I have learned over the years is that my own selfishness is at the root of most of the marital arguments we have, and I feel confident Lisa would agree that the quarrel we had on our honeymoon is no exception.

What I do remember is storming out of our condominium in Vail, Colorado, and having a good long discussion with the Lord out in the parking lot. By the time we were through, I was ready to go back inside and apologize. But, more importantly,

I made a firm resolution that I would never walk out on an argument with Lisa again but would do whatever it took, for as long as it took, to work things out.

The next set of lyrics from the Song of Songs tells a similar story. Not long after they were married—maybe while they were still on their honeymoon—Israel's newlyweds had a fight. As we listen to their song and hear about their painful separation, we discover that their marriage wasn't exactly "happily ever after." But, more importantly, as we see what it took for them to get back together, we learn how to fight valiantly for the romantic friendship that God calls marriage.

Not Tonight, Dear

The scene opens with the bride alone in her bed, half asleep, which helps to explain why the passage has a dreamlike quality. Apparently, her husband has been away from home—we're not sure why. He comes home late, only to find that the door to his bedchamber is locked. When his wife hears him knocking at the door, she says, "I slept, but my heart was awake. A sound! My beloved is knocking" (5:2).

As his wife lies in bed, her beloved husband tries to sweet-talk her into opening the door:

> Open to me, my sister, my love,
>   my dove, my perfect one,
> for my head is wet with dew,
>   my locks with the drops of the night. (5:2)

Speaking with sweet affection, the husband uses the same terms of endearment that we have heard before. As far as he is concerned, their honeymoon is far from over. The groom has come back home with a heart of love, and also the clear expectation that his bride will be ready for sexual intimacy—as ready as he is. His tender words contain more than enough innuendo to make his intentions clear.

Unfortunately for him, sex is the last thing that his wife has in mind. She was ready for that hours ago, when she took a bath and slipped into something a little more provocative. But the moment has passed, and all she wants to do now is stay in bed. So when she confides in her readers, she justifies her passive-aggressive behavior with a flimsy excuse: "I had put off my garment, how could I put it on? I had bathed my feet; how could I soil them?" (5:3).

Meanwhile, her husband is persistent; he keeps rattling the doorknob. And she is so in love with him that it doesn't take long for her to stop making him beg:

> My beloved put his hand to the latch,
>   and my heart was thrilled within me.
> I arose to open to my beloved,
>   and my hands dripped with myrrh,
> my fingers with liquid myrrh,
>   on the handles of the bolt. (5:4–5)

In other words, the young bride got out of bed, put on more perfume, and went to open the door, fully expecting that her beloved would fall into her arms and that they would go, once more, to bed. But when she opened the door, she received the shock of her life: her husband was nowhere in sight.

Does this lover's quarrel sound familiar? Anyone who has ever been in love knows that what Shakespeare said is true: "The course of true love never did run smooth."[1] He has his expectations; she has hers. And when their expectations aren't in sync, somebody gets angry. One spouse is ready for some form of intimacy; the other person isn't. It hurts to get pushed away, so by the time the reluctant partner is ready, the offended party wants to dish out the same kind of hurt that he (or she) received.

What happens to lovers all the time seems to be what happened to the lovers in the Song of Songs. It didn't take long for the bride to open her arms again to her beloved groom, but he was too selfish to wait. "I'll show her!" he said. "If she doesn't open this door and let me in right now, I'll go somewhere else." Instead of staying to work things out, he went away angry.

The lover's quarrel in Song of Songs 5 can help us see the patterns of selfishness that shape most of our own conflicts. When I get angry, it is often because I had an expectation that someone else failed to meet or maybe that life itself has failed to meet. In order to deal with my anger, it helps me to examine my expectations to see what they were and to ask whether they were directed to the glory of God or not. It will also help me to consider what expectations other people had, because that will probably help me be more sympathetic to their point of view, and it might help us figure out together how to make things right. Unless we examine our expectations in the clear light of God's Word, we will keep having the same arguments over and over again, and our relationship might not make it.

In Hot Pursuit

Imagine how devastated this young bride must have felt to open the door and find that her husband was gone. Not surprisingly, she was completely undone. Her heart was almost broken. "My soul failed me," she said (5:6).

In that awful moment, the young woman had a choice to make. One option was to slam the door, shut the latch, and say, "Forget him! He can sleep outside, for all I care. If he comes crawling back to me, then maybe I'll think about letting him in. But otherwise I am so through with this relationship!" This attitude is tempting for all of us, in almost every conflict we have. It is always easier to walk away. It is easier to wait for someone else to make the first move or to think about what the other person ought to do than what we can do to make the situation better. It is easier to expect an apology than to make one.

That is not what this woman did, however. As soon as she realized that her beloved was gone, she started looking for him: "I sought him, but found him not; I called him, but he gave no answer" (5:6). There was not a moment to lose. In hot pursuit, heedless of all danger, she went out in the dead of night to search the city streets. Her only concern was to find her husband. What courage! Even when the man she loved wasn't man enough to say that he was sorry, she was willing to fight for their relationship.

Sadly, our beautiful bride came to harm that night, at the hands of the very people who were charged to protect her and should have helped her file some sort of missing person report:

> The watchmen found me
> as they went about in the city;
> they beat me, they bruised me,
> they took away my veil,
> those watchmen of the walls. (5:7)

This verse raises all kinds of questions; we wish the Bible told us more. What the woman says hearkens back to the dream sequence in chapter 3, when she also went out to look for her beloved. Many commentators interpret chapter 5 as a dream too. But the fears it expresses are all too real. The woman went out to look for her husband, presumably still in her nightclothes. Given her state of undress, the local authorities assumed the worst about her character. Rather than helping her and protecting her, they violated her.

The Song of Songs does not dwell on this point; the story moves on. But we may pause to lament the terrible evils of physical abuse and sexual violence against women and to acknowledge that the temptation of brutality—including from people who are in charge of protecting people—is as old as human civilization. We long for a day when every woman is safe to go wherever she wants, either alone or in company, whether by day or by night, without any fear of coming to harm. Since that is not likely to happen on this side of glory, we need to do everything we can to protect women, especially those who are vulnerable or alone.

Friends and Lovers

Before we see how this story ends—a story that began in the safety of a private bedroom and then took a dark turn in the city streets—we need to see what motivated our brave and beautiful bride to fight for her marriage. What was the source of her passion?

Simply this: she had made a commitment to love. The vows the new bride had taken did not give her the freedom to run away at the first sign of trouble or to leave when something better came along. This marriage was "for better for worse, for richer for poorer, in sickness and in health, till death do us part."

After her painful encounter with the local watchmen, the country bride appealed to her city cousins. Even after what she had suffered at the hands of unjust men, she was not about to abandon her quest. But she knew that she needed help. So she called out to her bridal party, the chorus of young virgins who have had a voice in this drama from the beginning. She said,

"I adjure you, O daughters of Jerusalem, if you find my beloved, that you tell him I am sick with love" (5:8).

The daughters of Jerusalem are surprised at what the young bride says, and before they are willing to help, they have an important question that they want her to answer. Frankly, they wonder if her husband is really worth it. After all, he has just walked out on their relationship. He is so selfish that a little sexual frustration is all it takes for him to start breaking her heart. So they want to know what makes him so special:

> What is your beloved more than another beloved,
>   O most beautiful among women?
> What is your beloved more than another beloved,
>   that you thus adjure us? (5:9)

In reply, the woman bursts into song and gives her beloved the same kind of praise he had given to her back at the beginning of chapter 4. "Behold, you are beautiful, my love," he had said, "behold, you are beautiful!" (4:1). On that occasion, he proceeded to work his way down from her eyes to her breasts, comparing her beauty to quiet doves, juicy pomegranates, gentle fawns, and so on (4:2–7).

His wife reciprocates in chapter 5, using metaphor, simile, and hyperbole to describe her lover's anatomy. He is pure gold from head to toe:

> My beloved is radiant and ruddy,
>   distinguished among ten thousand.
> His head is the finest gold;
>   his locks are wavy,
>   black as a raven.
> His eyes are like doves
>   beside streams of water,

bathed in milk,
    sitting beside a full pool.
His cheeks are like beds of spices,
    mounds of sweet-smelling herbs.
His lips are lilies,
    dripping liquid myrrh.
His arms are rods of gold,
    set with jewels.
His body is polished ivory,
    bedecked with sapphires.
His legs are alabaster columns,
    set on bases of gold.
His appearance is like Lebanon,
    choice as the cedars.
His mouth is most sweet,
    and he is altogether desirable. (5:10–15)

If it sounds as though she is exaggerating, well, we have to make some allowances when people fall in love! Think of these verses as the first message that a young woman sends home to tell her mother about the amazing guy she met at college. If he has any flaws, she hasn't noticed them yet, or else she is willing to overlook them. As she quietly runs her eyes over his body, she likes what she sees. His handsome face, his beautiful eyes, the architecture of his strong arms and sturdy legs, his sweet lips—what's not to like?

Notice that the emblematic blazon in chapter 5 forms a nicely matched pair with the one we read in chapter 4. Both the bride and the groom see what is best and most beautiful in their beloved. Their compliments are complementary and their praise is equal, if not identical. They both need to be affirmed by the other person—as we all do—and they are both generous in giving such affirmation. The wife's praise is particularly striking because there is almost nothing like this in ancient literature: a song where a woman praises a man's physical form.

Perhaps the most important thing the woman says comes at the end of her song, when she puts into words something we have sensed all the way through the Song of Songs, even if no one has come right out and said it: "This is my beloved and this is my friend, O daughters of Jerusalem" (5:16).

Here the Bible unlocks the secret of a happy marriage by uniting friendship with romance. Make no mistake: these two people are lovers. They are so passionately in love with one another that they have united their bodies as well as their souls. We could sense their sexual chemistry from the very beginning of their duet, when the woman said that she wanted to be kissed with the man's kisses.

But these two lovers are also friends. Indeed, they are best friends. The word the woman uses to describe their friendship could also be used for a comrade-at-arms—someone you trust enough to go with you into any battle. Because of the strength of their companionship, this bride and this groom are both able to say, "I married my best friend." They are in a torrid romance that happens to be a total life partnership.

Every truly happy marriage has both of these dimensions: romance and friendship. It doesn't matter too much where couples begin. Sometimes they feel as if they are falling in love, but they hardly know one another yet. Their friendship needs to catch up with their romance, or else this won't be the right relationship for either one of them.

On the other hand, sometimes a man and a woman are friends for a while before they fall in love. I think of a couple from our church back in Philadelphia. A man befriended a woman who was facing significant challenges and needed practical help. He served her simply out of the goodness of his heart. Neither of them entered the relationship with any romantic expectation. But as time went on, their friendship grew. One day as they were standing next to each other in church, singing, their hands inadvertently touched. The moment was electric; they couldn't let go. As they clasped one another's hands, their friendship was recognized as a romance, and they both knew that they would never, ever let go of this relationship. And so they became husband and wife.

Every love story is different. There are many pathways that lead to covenant matrimony. The point is that the biblical pattern for a healthy marriage is romantic friendship. By itself, neither friendship nor romance is sufficient. In order to move forward in a marriage partnership, couples need to be able to say, "This is my lover" and also "this is my friend."

Reunited, and It Feels So Good

Given the strength of this couple's partnership, it is not surprising that their lovers' quarrel had a happy ending.

The bridal chorus listened carefully to the bride's song of praise for her beloved friend. Once their questions were answered and they knew for sure how much she loved her husband, they were ready to help find him. They sang a little song to ask where she had last seen him:

> Where has your beloved gone,
>   O most beautiful among women?
> Where has your beloved turned,
>   that we may seek him with you? (6:1)

We really don't know where the young bride found her beloved, or exactly what happened next, but all of a sudden he was right there beside her. Songs are like that. Dreams are like that too: they provide vivid pictures, but they don't necessarily give all the details. In this case, all we know is that soon the bride and the groom went back to their bedchamber, which she describes as a garden of delight:

> My beloved has gone down to his garden
>   to the beds of spices,
> to graze in the gardens
>   and to gather lilies. (6:2)

In their beautiful garden, the newlyweds will enjoy the best part of any marital conflict: the part where they "kiss and make up," renewing their relationship sexually as well as emotionally. In the heat of their conflict, they had treated sex as something to take or to use—even to use against each other. But now, in the heat of their passion, they rediscover God's design for sexual intimacy in marriage, which is self-giving.

There is much wisdom in traditional wedding vows, in which the bride and the groom say, "With my body, I thee worship." Israel's newlyweds had made similar promises. They belonged to one another—body and soul—by the unbreakable bond of sacred wedding vows. So the wife ends her song by once again celebrating their mutual possession: "I am my beloved's, and my beloved is mine" (Song 6:3).

Savior, Lover, Friend

This relationship was worth fighting for, as every God-centered marriage is. One of the best examples I know happened during my first months at Oxford University. I had done something wrong—something I was deeply ashamed of. As a matter of my conscience before God, I needed to tell Lisa what I had done, but I was too ashamed to do it in person. So I wrote her a letter, left it on the shelf, and mentioned it on my way out the door. Then I left our flat as fast as I could and went out into the city, too upset to study.

Lisa got about halfway through the letter and started after me. She didn't know exactly where I was going. I'm a fast walker, so I had a good head start. Also, she was about seven months pregnant. But in the providence of God she found me about a mile away, in front of a store on Broad Street. She wanted me to know right away how much she loved me, so she ran up and gave me a huge hug. Tears were streaming down both our faces. We made quite a spectacle, especially given how reserved most Brits are. Then she said something I'll never forget: "What, did you think I didn't know that you were a sinner?" In that moment I was confronted with the fresh perspective I needed. I was accepted without qualification, forgiven without question, and loved without reservation by my best friend in the whole world.

Know this: you have a Savior who loves you with the same kind of love, to infinite perfection. He started to show you his love when he came knocking on the door to your heart (see Rev. 3:20). Even when you turned your back on him—more than once—he came looking for you. Heedless of all danger, he was willing to endure every kind of abuse, up to and including crucifixion. To personalize one good old hymn, "From heaven He came and sought you, to be His holy bride; with His own blood He bought you, and for your life He died."[2]

Knowing exactly what kind of sinner you are, Jesus nevertheless was willing to fight for your love all the way to the cross.

He did this because he loves you, because he sees the beauty in you, and because he wants to have a relationship with you that will go on and on forever. This is your Lover. This is your Friend.

When you experience the loving friendship of Jesus Christ, you are free to become the kind of lover who isn't selfish and the kind of friend who doesn't run away from a conflict. Instead, you do everything you can to make things right with the people you love, no matter what the cost.

6

The Duet after the Fight

You are beautiful as Tirzah, my love,
    lovely as Jerusalem,
    awesome as an army with banners.
Turn away your eyes from me,
    for they overwhelm me—
Your hair is like a flock of goats
    leaping down the slopes of Gilead.
Your teeth are like a flock of ewes
    that have come up from the washing;
all of them bear twins;
    not one among them has lost its young.
Your cheeks are like halves of a pomegranate
    behind your veil.
There are sixty queens and eighty concubines,
    and virgins without number.
My dove, my perfect one, is the only one,
    the only one of her mother,
    pure to her who bore her.
The young women saw her and called her blessed;
    the queens and concubines also, and they praised her.

"Who is this who looks down like the dawn,
    beautiful as the moon, bright as the sun,
    awesome as an army with banners?"

I went down to the nut orchard
    to look at the blossoms of the valley,
to see whether the vines had budded,
    whether the pomegranates were in bloom.
Before I was aware, my desire set me
    among the chariots of my kinsman, a prince.

Return, return, O Shulammite,
    return, return, that we may look upon you.

Why should you look upon the Shulammite,
    as upon a dance before two armies?

How beautiful are your feet in sandals,
    O noble daughter!
Your rounded thighs are like jewels,
    the work of a master hand.
Your navel is a rounded bowl
    that never lacks mixed wine.
Your belly is a heap of wheat,
    encircled with lilies.
Your two breasts are like two fawns,
    twins of a gazelle.
Your neck is like an ivory tower.
Your eyes are pools in Heshbon,
    by the gate of Bath-rabbim.
Your nose is like a tower of Lebanon,
    which looks toward Damascus.
Your head crowns you like Carmel,
    and your flowing locks are like purple;
    a king is held captive in the tresses.

How beautiful and pleasant you are,
    O loved one, with all your delights!

Your stature is like a palm tree,
    and your breasts are like its clusters.
I say I will climb the palm tree
    and lay hold of its fruit.
Oh may your breasts be like clusters of the vine,
    and the scent of your breath like apples,
and your mouth like the best wine.

It goes down smoothly for my beloved,
    gliding over lips and teeth.

I am my beloved's,
    and his desire is for me.

Come, my beloved,
    let us go out into the fields
    and lodge in the villages;
let us go out early to the vineyards
    and see whether the vines have budded,
whether the grape blossoms have opened
    and the pomegranates are in bloom.
There I will give you my love.
The mandrakes give forth fragrance,
    and beside our doors are all choice fruits,
new as well as old,
    which I have laid up for you, O my beloved.

Oh that you were like a brother to me
    who nursed at my mother's breasts!
If I found you outside, I would kiss you,
    and none would despise me.
I would lead you and bring you
    into the house of my mother—
    she who used to teach me.

I would give you spiced wine to drink,
the juice of my pomegranate.
His left hand is under my head,
and his right hand embraces me!
I adjure you, O daughters of Jerusalem,
that you not stir up or awaken love
until it pleases. (Song 6:4–8:4)

It takes only one person to forgive, but it takes at least two people to reconcile. This is the basic difference between forgiveness and reconciliation.

Forgiveness can be unilateral. Even if one person never says, "I'm sorry," the person who has been wronged can still choose to offer forgiveness in the name of Jesus. This is what happened in Charleston, South Carolina, when a member of the historic Emanuel African Methodist Episcopal Church publicly forgave the man who murdered her mother, her pastor, and seven other members of her church family during a Wednesday-night Bible study. "I forgive you," said Nadine Collier. "You took something very precious away from me. I will never get to talk to her ever again—but I forgive you, and have mercy on your soul."[1] Without ever receiving any apology, Collier offered forgiveness simply through the power of the cross.

Reconciliation, on the other hand, requires a double work of grace. For a broken relationship to be fully reconciled, sin must be confessed and forgiven—sometimes on both sides. Although forgiveness can be performed as a solo, reconciliation is always sung as a duet.

The love songs in the Song of Songs include the lyrics for a duet of reconciliation. It happened like this. A young couple fell in love at first sight and began a passionate courtship. Because true love waits, before getting married they sought the support of their spiritual community, including their parents. They exchanged their wedding vows, in which they promised to belong to one another forever. Then they went off on their honeymoon, during which—unfortunately—the two of them had a big fight. But when the groom walked away, his bride went to look for him until she found him—her lover and her friend. So the romance was reconciled. When last we saw our newlyweds, they were together again in the garden of love, where the bride was singing, "I am my beloved's, and my beloved is mine" (6:3).

What we haven't heard yet is what the groom has to say in response. We know where his wife stands, because she has sung his praises from head to toe: his wavy locks, his dreamy eyes, his lily lips, his golden feet (5:10–16). But how does her husband feel about her? Is this only the solo of forgiveness, or is it the duet of reconciliation? And what does this song teach us, whether we are married or single, about healing the broken relationships in our own lives?

You Are My Only One

After a huge fight such as these newlyweds had, some husbands would be tempted to hold a grudge. They would be grumpy because their wives didn't jump right out of bed to answer the door. Or they would be so critical that even though they got back together again, the wife would be left feeling that the conflict was mostly her fault. Giving someone the cold shoulder, blaming the other person for what happened, feeling morally superior—these attitudes are tempting in all of our conflicts, even when they get somewhat resolved.

That is not what this husband does, however. Instead of scolding her, he gives her the same lavish praise that he had for her when they first fell in love. His passion is undimmed:

> You are beautiful as Tirzah, my love,
>   lovely as Jerusalem,
>   awesome as an army with banners.
> Turn away your eyes from me,
>   for they overwhelm me—
> Your hair is like a flock of goats
>   leaping down the slopes of Gilead.
> Your teeth are like a flock of ewes
>   that have come up from the washing;
> all of them bear twins;
>   not one among them has lost its young.
> Your cheeks are like halves of a pomegranate
>   behind your veil. (6:4–7)

We have heard most of this before: her flowing hair, her perfect white teeth, her pomegranate cheeks (4:1–5). Nevertheless, all of it bears repeating. We might say that the way to a woman's heart is through her ears. By speaking words of appreciation and affection, the husband gives his wife the deep sense of security that comes from knowing he sees her beauty. This is something to say not only once but repeatedly, especially when a couple is trying to reconcile. A wife needs to know that her husband still sees her the way that he saw her when they first fell in love.

By addressing his wife directly, the husband shows that their reconciliation is real. Earlier, when she spoke about reconciliation, she was not speaking with her husband but talking to her friends—her bridal chorus, the daughters of Jerusalem.

But now husband and wife are speaking face-to-face, which is where the husband lingers. He will get to the rest of her later, but he wants to speak to her soul before he touches her body. Iain Duguid writes, "Since the conflict was over sex to begin with, he wishes to reassure her that he is not merely interested in getting her to sleep with him again; it is their face-to-face relationship that he wishes to see fully restored."[2]

What is new in these verses is the groom's growing respect for his wife's unique strength. Remember, she was willing to brave the dangers of the night to go out and look for him up and down some dangerous streets. So now he compares her to Tirzah and Jerusalem, the capital cities of Israel and Judah, and says that she is "awesome as an army with banners" (6:4, 10). Evidently, the more he gets to know her, the more he is in awe of her: "She has a mysterious power over him that he finds both fascinating and terrifying."[3]

Something else is new here too, and that is the husband's appreciation for his bride's uniqueness. There is no one else like this woman in the entire world. As far as he is concerned, she is the perfect woman for him:

> There are sixty queens and eighty concubines,
>   and virgins without number.
> My dove, my perfect one, is the only one,
>   the only one of her mother,
>   pure to her who bore her.
> The young women saw her and called her blessed;
>   the queens and concubines also, and they praised her.
>   (6:8–9)

The reference to queens and concubines obviously calls Solomon to mind—the king whose vast harem eventually boasted seven hundred wives and three hundred concubines (1 Kings 11:3). But the husband in the Song of Songs wisely values quality over quantity. He is a one-woman man, and thus his wife is as irreplaceable to him as an only daughter. In her purity and perfection, she is the only one for him.

Here it is good to remember that the Song of Songs operates simultaneously on at least two different levels. This book is an album of love songs about a man and a woman who fall in love, get married, and then need to work hard at their relationship. But their marriage also teaches us about Christ and the church, as every true love story does. We know this because the Bible repeatedly draws explicit comparisons between human-level romance and our love relationship with the living God.

In the spiritual mystery of our marriage to Christ, Jesus is a one-woman man, so to speak. He has never wavered in his affection for his people—for everyone who belongs to him by faith. As imperfect as we are, he sees us as the perfect people for him. So whenever there is a breach in our relationship—which is always our fault, never his—he comes to us again and tells us how beautiful we are, how much he loves us, and how pure we are in his sight. Jesus gives us every reassurance that even after everything we have done wrong, we are still the object of his affection.

If seeing ourselves this way seems like a stretch, or even downright dishonest, then we need to remember the power of God's gracious love, which accepts us as we are and then makes us more and more like what we ought to become. We also need to believe the promise that he gave us through the prophet Isaiah: "You shall be called My Delight Is in Her . . . for the Lord delights in you. . . . And as the bridegroom rejoices over the bride, so shall your God rejoice over you" (Isa. 62:4–5).

Can you receive this good word, even in your brokenness, that you are beloved by God?

Prince Charming

Soon the groom will have more to say. But before he speaks again, Song of Songs 6 ends with the words of his beloved bride and of her attendants:

> I went down to the nut orchard
> to look at the blossoms of the valley,
> to see whether the vines had budded,
> whether the pomegranates were in bloom.
> Before I was aware, my desire set me
> among the chariots of my kinsman, a prince.
> Return, return, O Shulammite,
> return, return, that we may look upon you. (6:11–13)

If we wish to do so, we can probably find some double entendres here, expressing sexual desire. But we shouldn't miss the overall motif of fruitfulness. The long-awaited season for love has returned (see 2:10–13), and the newlywed bride is hoping it will blossom and bear fruit. In the ancient world, the pomegranate was known not for being rich in antioxidants, as it is today, but for being packed with large seeds. Thus it serves as the ideal image for a large family. As this marriage begins to flower, the young bride is looking ahead to the blessing of many offspring.

And why not? She really is married to the perfect man, so naturally she wants to bear his children. Verse 12 is notoriously difficult to translate, but what is unmistakable is the high honor that the young woman gives to the man whose love has elevated her life. She calls him her "prince." Here is how

Iain Duguid explains the verse: "Her fears that she had lost the man forever were false: he still loved her, in spite of her earlier coldness. When she heard the man's words and discovered that he still found her uniquely attractive, she was as enraptured as if she had been caught up in a royal chariot with Prince Charming."[4]

Some scholars see the courtly language in these verses as a sign that the Song of Songs tells us the story of King Solomon. We have mentioned this interpretation before, but I have also indicated that I read the Song somewhat differently. I think it uses royal titles to show the high and proper dignity of this couple, and every couple. If it is true that God is our Father, and that he is also a great King, then we are all—every one of us—his royal offspring. This makes us all princes and princesses in the kingdom of God. It also makes it natural for a loving wife to see her beloved husband as a kind of prince.

We see our exalted status in God's kingdom perhaps most clearly at a wedding, when a bride and the groom dress in royal splendor, almost as if they were king and queen for a day. When they do this, they are not playing "make believe" but presenting themselves as they truly are. Maybe we should wear wedding clothes all the time or walk around in crowns and tiaras. This is who we were always meant to be: the royal children of God, the rightful heirs of his everlasting kingdom.

I Want You, Babe

At this point, Israel's newlyweds—Prince Charming and his Snow White bride—are well on their way to reconciliation. This includes, of course, the renewal of their relationship sexually. I say "of course" because sharing sex is almost always part of what it means for a married couple to resolve a conflict.

Their reunion as one flesh is something that both bride and groom mention in their song. By comparing his wife to the dancing women who celebrated military victories in ancient Israel (see, e.g., Ex. 15:19–21; 1 Sam. 18:6–7), the young husband declares that she is the center of his attention. The conflict is over, two enemies are reconciled, and all eyes are on the victory dance: "Why should you look upon the Shulammite, as upon a dance before two armies?" (Song 6:13).

Once again, the groom sings the beauty of his bride. This time, however, he starts with her feet and works his way up her body:

> How beautiful are your feet in sandals,
>   O noble daughter!
> Your rounded thighs are like jewels,
>   the work of a master hand.
> Your navel is a rounded bowl
>   that never lacks mixed wine.
> Your belly is a heap of wheat,
>   encircled with lilies.
> Your two breasts are like two fawns,
>   twins of a gazelle.
> Your neck is like an ivory tower.
> Your eyes are pools in Heshbon,
>   by the gate of Bath-rabbim.
> Your nose is like a tower of Lebanon,
>   which looks toward Damascus.
> Your head crowns you like Carmel,
>   and your flowing locks are like purple;
>   a king is held captive in the tresses. (7:1–5)

Although this description is physical, it is not primarily visual. By mentioning heaps of wheat and towers of ivory, the husband does not tell us what his wife looks like in any literal way but draws deeper connections. He celebrates a beauty that is more than skin deep. He also recognizes that his wife is God's handiwork. When he says that her body is "the work of a master hand" (7:1), he is admiring God's exceptional craftsmanship. The way this woman is put together—not just physically, but her total personhood—is a gift from God.

The husband's words in the Song of Songs invite us to see every woman as she truly is: a divine masterpiece. Presumably some of his points of comparison were more flattering in ancient Israel than they would be today. Telling a woman that her nose is "like a tower of Lebanon" seems especially ill-advised (7:4). But without crossing the line between the erotic and the pornographic, this man tells his wife that her curves are in all the right places. Indeed, he sees her body as the Promised Land, which probably explains why he uses place names from Israel to describe it.

We should be sure to notice that this song is not just about sex. The husband chooses his words carefully to echo some of the things that his wife had said previously. By speaking of her nobility (only the daughters of wealthy people wore sandals in those days), by putting a crown on her head, and by adorning her with royal purple, he shows her the same honor that she showed to him when she called him a prince. They both see the nobility in one another. Also, by using images of fertility—piles of wheat and bowls of wine—he communicates his openness to the gift of children. Thus his words affirm her heart's desires. This is a vital part of full reconciliation, being sensitive and receptive to what another person wants.

But make no mistake: this song *is* about sex. The husband wants to do more than talk. He wants to make love to the woman he loves:

How beautiful and pleasant you are,
O loved one, with all your delights!
Your stature is like a palm tree,
and your breasts are like its clusters.
I say I will climb the palm tree
and lay hold of its fruit.
Oh may your breasts be like clusters of the vine,
and the scent of your breath like apples,
and your mouth like the best wine. (7:6–9)

The bride's beauty is so intoxicating that her husband wants to get close enough to touch her, to smell her, to kiss her . . .

The Meanings of Marriage

At this point, the woman suddenly joins the love song, adding her harmony to his melody. As her husband kisses and caresses her, she plants a kiss right on his lips and sings to their pleasure—not just her pleasure, but also his. "It goes down smoothly for my beloved," she tells us, "gliding over lips and teeth" (7:9). Then she celebrates once again the mutual possession and shared self-giving of their marital bond: "I am my beloved's, and his desire is for me" (7:10; cf. 2:16; 6:3). This song is not a solo. It is definitely a duet in which vows are renewed, romance is reconciled, and sexual intimacy is shared.

The word "desire" in verse 10 is an echo from Eden. Back in Genesis 3, when our first parents committed the first sin, God told the woman that her "desire" would be for her husband (v. 16)—not her sexual desire, in all likelihood, but her desire to have the upper hand in their relationship. For his part, the man would try to "rule" over her (v. 16)—not by servant leadership but through superior force. This perpetual battle of the sexes was the consequence of sin. But here the curse has been reversed. The husband's desire is no longer to dominate but to give himself in love. For her part, the wife's desire is to bless her husband. They both want to treat each other the way that a man and a woman should, the way that God always intended.

As the duet continues, the wife tells her husband what else she wants out of this romance. The intimacy she desires is not only sexual but also relational. She wants his friendship and companionship. For her, this starts with a return to the countryside of her childhood, where she can visit the places she loves with the person who has become her life partner. This is an important aspect of almost every romance—sharing the background that makes us who we are. For the lover in the Song of Songs, the invitation for her husband to experience the things that she enjoyed growing up goes like this:

> Come, my beloved,
> let us go out into the fields,
> and lodge in the villages;
> let us go out early to the vineyards
> and see whether the vines have budded,
> whether the grape blossoms have opened
> and the pomegranates are in bloom. (7:11–12)

Another thing this woman wants to share with her beloved is her family, and hopefully then to receive their blessing:

> Oh that you were like a brother to me
> who nursed at my mother's breasts!
> If I found you outside, I would kiss you,
> and none would despise me.
> I would leave you and bring you
> into the house of my mother—
> she who used to teach me. (8:1–2)

What may sound strange to our modern ears is the bride's desire for her husband to be like a brother to her—someone who grew up with her in her mother's house. This echoes the sibling language that her husband used when he called her his "sister" as well as his "bride" (e.g., 4:9–10). Today, if a woman says that she wants to treat a man like a brother, this is sure to suck the romance right out of their relationship. Social customs were different in ancient Israel, however. In those days, respectable couples generally did not make public displays of their affection—not even husbands and wives. But blood relations were permitted to embrace outside the home. This bride wished that she had such freedom. Then she could show the world how much she loved her husband, right out in the open.

She also wanted their friendship to be fruitful. The flowers and various fruits throughout the Song of Songs are symbols of fertility and signs that the season for lovemaking has come. At the end of chapter 7 and beginning of chapter 8 the bride mentions two love-fruits that symbolize the blessing of children specifically: "The mandrakes give forth fragrance, and beside our doors are all choice fruits, new as well as old, which I have laid up for you, O my beloved. . . . I would give you spiced wine to drink, the juice of my pomegranate" (7:13; 8:2). Both mandrakes and pomegranates were associated with making love and having large families in the ancient world. Thus the fruit that decorated their honeymoon suite shows that the happy couple hopes to have a family. Their marriage is open to the gift of children, as every God-honoring marriage should be.

This last point is worth emphasizing in a culture that sometimes sees children as a burden, or where young couples regard parenthood as an obstacle to achieving their goals in life. To be sure, having children is not the be-all and end-all of human experience. Indeed, parenthood is mainly a call to lifelong sacrifice. But the Bible consistently regards children as a gift from the Lord (e.g., Ps. 127:3). Procreation is one of God's primary purposes for marriage (Mal. 2:15), as part of his plan for populating the world and building up a kingdom. Training children to worship the Lord is one of the primary responsibilities of every generation (Ps. 145:4). Thus every Christian marriage ought to be wide open to the gift of sons and daughters.

Openness to children is part of seeing the big picture of God's purposes for marriage. Although the German theologian Dietrich Bonhoeffer was never married, he did get engaged, and as a single man he thought deeply about the meaning of marriage. During his last days in a Nazi prison, he handwrote a beautiful sermon for his niece Renate Schleicher and his close friend Eberhard Bethge, to be read at their wedding. Here is what Bonhoeffer said about the wider purposes of covenant matrimony:

> Marriage is more than your love for each other. It has a higher dignity and power, for it is God's holy ordinance, through which He wills to perpetuate the human race till the end of time. In your love you see only your two selves in the world, but in marriage you are a link in the chain of the generations, which God causes to come and to pass away to His glory, and calls into His kingdom. In your love, you see only the heaven of your own happiness, but in marriage you are placed at a post of responsibility towards the world and mankind. Your love is your own private possession, but marriage is more than something personal—it is a status, an office. Just as it is the crown, and not merely the will to rule, that makes the king, so it is marriage, and not merely your love for each other, that joins you together in the sight of God and man.[5]

The End of the Affair

All of these desires are included in God's multiple purposes for marriage: intimacy, companionship, friendship, sex, children, and family. But none of this would have been possible for Israel's newlyweds unless they were willing and able to reconcile their differences. After all the beautiful metaphors, the duet ends with something literal: "His left hand is under my head, and his right hand embraces me" (Song 8:3).

This has been the woman's desire from the very first verse of the Song of Songs, to be totally embraced by the man she loves—the man who promised to love her to the end of their days. She is not shy about saying that she wants him as badly as he wants her. But this was not a selfish desire. Listen carefully to what she says: "I will give you my love" (7:12).

This simple verse speaks volumes about God's design for sex inside of marriage. By putting these words in the woman's mouth, the Holy Spirit affirms her sexual desire. Maybe this seems obvious, but it hasn't always seemed obvious to the Christian church. The holy gift of sex is as much for a woman as it is for a man. The proper thing for both husbands and wives to do with this gift is not to take it but to give it. So the woman in the Song of Songs declares her desire to give her husband all of her love, and all of herself, including her body.

The better we understand these simple principles, the more things will fall into place for us. Instead of thinking of sex as something to *have*, which is exactly the wrong verb, we will think of it as something to *give*, or maybe to *share*. Suddenly it becomes clear why masturbation will not help us, but only hinder us. Sexual pleasure is something that God intends for us not to give ourselves but to offer generously to someone else. Habits of self-gratification always make us more selfish—of course they do. Is this what we really want? Or do we want to fight with everything we have—by every power of the Holy Spirit—to become a man or a woman whose life overflows with more self-giving love?

We see the pattern of self-giving love most clearly in the saving grace of Jesus Christ. When Jesus found his beloved bride, the church, he chose to love her forever. Rather than taking something from her, he wanted to give her himself—all of himself. So he offered his body for her unto death. The cross is the gift of Christ's love, which reconciles us to God and gives us an everlasting song to sing. This song is not a solo, but a duet—the love song that we sing with our Savior.

Once we fall in love with Jesus, our deepest desire is to give ourselves to him. To paraphrase the famous first answer from the Heidelberg Catechism, by faith we belong—body and soul—to our faithful husband, Jesus Christ. For that very reason, because we belong to Jesus, we will do everything we can to be reconciled to one another. We are—all of us—made for one another, as well as for God. The duet we sing with our Divine Redeemer gives us the melody and the harmony to sing in all our human relationships as well. By his grace we are able to forgive, and through his Spirit we can be reconciled.

7

Forever Yours

Who is that coming up from the wilderness,
    leaning on her beloved?

Under the apple tree I awakened you.
There your mother was in labor with you;
    there she who bore you was in labor.

Set me as a seal upon your heart,
    as a seal upon your arm,
for love is strong as death,
    jealousy is fierce as the grave.
Its flashes are flashes of fire,
    the very flame of the LORD.
Many waters cannot quench love,
    neither can floods drown it.
If a man offered for love
    all the wealth of his house,
    he would be utterly despised.

We have a little sister,
    and she has no breasts.
What shall we do for our sister
    on the day when she is spoken for?

If she is a wall,
we will build on her a battlement of silver,
but if she is a door,
we will enclose her with boards of cedar.

I was a wall,
and my breasts were like towers;
then I was in his eyes
as one who finds peace.

Solomon had a vineyard at Baal-hamon;
he let out the vineyard to keepers;
each one was to bring for its fruit a thousand pieces of silver.
My vineyard, my very own, is before me;
you, O Solomon, may have the thousand,
and the keepers of the fruit two hundred.

O you who dwell in the gardens,
with companions listening for your voice;
let me hear it.

Make haste, my beloved,
and be like a gazelle
or a young stag
on the mountains of spices. (Song 8:5–14)

Benjamin Breckinridge Warfield ranks in the first tier of American theologians. For more than thirty years Warfield taught systematic theology at Princeton Seminary. The numerous columns and book reviews he published made him a household name across the country in the late nineteenth and early twentieth centuries, and his essays on the inspiration and inerrancy of Scripture, among many others, remain influential to this day.

What many people do not know is the story of B. B. Warfield's extraordinary devotion to his wife, Annie, through her many years of suffering. Warfield married at age twenty-five, and the happy couple traveled to Germany for their honeymoon. Tragically, they were caught in a severe thunderstorm, and Annie was struck by lightning. This traumatized Annie mentally and physically so severely that she was an invalid for the rest of her life. Warfield gently cared for his wife every day for the next forty years. In fact, he basically stayed in Princeton for the rest of their marriage, leaving home for only an hour or two at a time—mainly to lecture to his students—and rarely venturing farther away than walking distance.[1]

Warfield lovingly set aside time from his studies to read to Annie every day. People in town said that the great theologian "had only two interests in life—his work, and Mrs. Warfield."[2] In their tender affection for and faithful commitment to one another, the Warfields demonstrated the final truth claims of the Song of Songs: "Many waters cannot quench love," for "love is strong as death" (8:6–7).

The Family Tree

The happy couple that we have met in these biblical songs made the same life commitment by vowing to love each other with an undying love. At the end of their epithalamion—their beautiful wedding song—they celebrate their love as a gift from God and come together in an embrace that will never end.

The bride and the groom are not the only people in this story, however. For the people of God, marriage is not a personal achievement but a community project. So the last chapter of the Song of Songs is like the end of a musical, when all the characters come back on stage for the final number. As the performers recite their closing lines, they repeat many themes from earlier in the production. King Solomon is mentioned again in these verses, as are his vineyards. The bride's brothers return, for better or for worse. And when the bride speaks to her wedding attendants, she repeats a familiar admonition: "I adjure you, O daughters of Jerusalem, that you not stir up or awaken love until it pleases" (Song 8:4).

The bridal party responds with a declaration that sounds almost like the introduction of the bride and the groom at a wedding reception: "Who is that coming up from the wilderness," they ask, "leaning on her beloved?" (8:5). The answer, of course, is that a beautiful bride is making her entrance—the country girl who started this song by telling us about the man she hoped would kiss her "with the kisses of his mouth" (1:2).

The lover and the beloved have become husband and wife. When the young woman who is the star of this show first came up from the wilderness, she was all alone. But now the two of them are walking hand in hand. They are coming home, maybe after their honeymoon. She is leaning on her beloved—a gesture of intimacy and dependency. Clearly, their connection is more than physical. Indeed, the climax of their love story is not sexual but relational.

When the song started, both of the lovers in the Song of Songs were still single. But now we picture them walking through life side by side, leaning on each other's love, growing old together. They will share the kind of closeness that C. S. Lewis enjoyed with Joy Davidman when the happy couple married late in life—what Lewis described as "mere ease and ordinariness. . . . No need to talk. No need to make love. No needs at all except perhaps to stir the fire."[3] The martial artist and movie star Bruce Lee used a similar image to describe marital affection: "Love is like a friendship caught on fire. In the beginning a flame, very pretty, often hot and fierce, but still only light and flickering. As love grows older, our hearts mature and our love becomes as coals, deep-burning and unquenchable."[4]

In addition to expecting them to grow old together, we also expect Israel's newlyweds to start a family. This is signified by the return of the image of the apple tree. The bride says, "Under the apple tree I awakened you. There your mother was in labor with you; there she who bore you was in labor" (8:5). More than once the young woman has told her girlfriends not to arouse sexual desire until the time is right. But now that she is getting married the time has come—not just to awaken love but also to share that love sexually, and hopefully to receive the gift of children. The apple tree is not merely the trysting place where the couple sometimes met during their courtship; it has become the symbol of a solid and fruitful marriage. Metaphorically, it's the family tree—the place where mothers go into labor and give birth to their children.

To modern ears it may sound strange for these newlyweds to go back to the place where the husband was born. These days, most couples want to go out and make their own home. In fact, the last thing they want to do is go back and live with their in-laws! But in the biblical world it was common for extended families to live in close proximity.

Besides, this love affair has always been a family matter. Soon it would be time for another mother to go into labor and give birth. Underneath the apple tree, what started out as a romance would become the rising generation. The whole progression of life is captured in this single image, which is reminiscent of the rhyme that kids used to sing at my elementary school when they wanted to tease someone: "So-and-so and so-and-so, sittin' in a tree, K-I-S-S-I-N-G. First comes love, then comes marriage, then comes baby in a baby carriage."

This is all part of God's stunning design for human sexuality. What perpetuates the human race is the union of two souls who share their bodies to produce entirely new people. Their intercourse is intricately designed in a way that fosters intimacy, gives intense pleasure, and introduces new joy to the world. Amazing! If human sexuality happened to be the only thing that God ever invented, for that alone he would deserve as much praise as we could possibly give him.

Love's Climax

The Song of Songs was written to tell us that the divinely ordained context for sex is love—specifically, the love of a faithful God lived out in the love of a faithful marriage.

We live in a culture that does everything it can to separate sex from marriage. In fact, relationships have become so degraded that some young people try to separate the physical act of sex from their emotions. In the words of one interviewee from the University of Pennsylvania, "It's kind of like a spiral. The girls adapt a little bit, because they stop expecting that they're going to get a boyfriend—because if that's all you're trying to do, you're going to be miserable. But at the same time, they want to, like, have contact with guys. So they hook up and 'try not to get attached.'" The journalist who reported this interview commented that trying "not to get attached" is really a vain attempt to "divorce sex from *feeling*."[5]

Another sad example of our society's broken sexuality comes from Peggy Orenstein's research on the sexual experiences and attitudes of young women. One high school senior from Northern California told Orenstein, "I'll be hooking up with some guy who's really hot, then things get heavier and all of a sudden my mind shifts and I'm not a real person: it's like, This is me performing. This is me acting. . . . And I don't even know who it is I'm playing, who that 'she' actually is. It's some fantasy girl, I guess, maybe the girl from porn."[6]

One simple way to demonstrate our culture's attitude toward sex and marriage is to consider how much more frequently the people who have sexual relationships on television or in the movies are not married, at least to each other. By contrast, the love of God brings sex and marriage together. Thus the Bible consistently presents a loving marriage as the spiritual and hermeneutical context for sex.

The bride we meet in the Song of Songs celebrated her loving marriage in one of the finest love songs ever written. The lyrics go like this:

> Set me as a seal upon your heart,
>   as a seal upon your arm,
> for love is strong as death,
>   jealousy is fierce as the grave.
> Its flashes are flashes of fire,
>   the very flame of the LORD.
> Many waters cannot quench love,
>   neither can floods drown it.
> If a man offered for love
>   all the wealth of his house,
>   he would be utterly despised. (8:6–7)

This poem is as close as the Song of Songs ever gets to a definition of love. It asks, to what shall we compare the love that unites two souls as one flesh? Then it offers several answers, which together help us understand what the Bible means by *love*.

Love is like the clay cylinder or golden signet ring that a wealthy person wore as the invaluable proof of his or her unique identity. In the biblical world, such a seal would have been worn on a cord around someone's neck and used to sign official documents. In effect, a seal was someone's signature. Maybe the closest modern equivalent is the electronic chip on a high-tech credit card. What this bride wanted her husband to do was to take her seal and wear it around his neck, keeping her close to his heart; or else he could bind it to his arm, making a public display of their mutual commitment. Her seal would function the same way that wedding rings function today; it would show that she belonged to her beloved by the vows of covenant matrimony. It would also show that he was totally committed to her—with both the love of his heart and the strength of his arm.

We could also compare love to death. Is anything stronger? Death is immovable and irresistible. Who can fail to answer when it calls? Death has defeated great armies and conquered mighty kings. Indeed, it has already staked its claim on every one of us. When death finally lays its cold hand on someone, its grip will never let go.

If death is so powerful, then what love is of equal strength? No merely human love. Wedding vows are the most enduring promises that anyone can make, yet even they have their limits. Husbands and wives promise to love one another "till death us part," but no longer. The only love as strong as death, therefore, is the love of God. This explains why the Song of Songs claims a love that *is* as strong as death. The love described in these verses is a divine flame: "Its flashes are flashes of fire, the very flame of the LORD" (Song 8:6).

Here, for the first time in the entire Song of Songs, God is mentioned by name. His love is the strongest love. The song describes it as a jealous love, as fierce as the grave. We usually think of jealousy as something unattractive or even sinful. But when a relationship ought to be exclusive, then it is right to be jealous! Holy jealousy is the righteous refusal to share something that shouldn't be shared. This is the kind of exclusive love relationship that God wants to have with us. He doesn't want us to give our love to any other deity; he wants us to worship him alone. He wants this for our benefit, not his. So he loves us with a holy jealousy—the kind of jealousy that ought to protect a marriage, especially sexually.

True love is also unquenchable—what the Song of Songs defines as an eternal flame. Once our love is lit by God, the fire he starts is stronger than any flood. It cannot be washed away by the waters of stormy troubles or drowned by high waves of sorrow. Love is an almighty flame.

What would you be willing to pay for love this lasting, strong, and true? It doesn't matter, because love is not for sale. The kind of love that people sing about in the Song of Songs is priceless. Not even Solomon in all his splendor was rich enough to purchase it. In fact, the Song says that "if a man offered for love all the wealth of his house, he would be utterly despised" (8:7), which is the Bible's way of saying that "money can't buy you love." Love is not a commodity, but a free gift from the God of love. Here is how Iain Duguid paraphrased these verses: "Love cannot be bought and sold. It is a single-hearted, lifelong, jealous devotion between one man and one woman, from the moment it seizes a person until the moment of their death. Nothing but the grave can separate two people who are thus joined together."[7]

On Virginity

If a loving marriage is priceless—if the unquenchable flame that unites one man and one woman in one covenant for one lifetime is as strong as death—then we should do everything we can to protect sexual purity. This is the practical point that the Bible brings us to at the end of the Song of Songs.

Remember, Solomon's book is like an album of love songs. On this analogy, the eighth verse of the eighth chapter begins a new track. The new song in this Bible passage seems to be sung by the bride's older brothers, whom we first met back in chapter 1 when they kept their sister out working in the fields. Apparently, now they are trying to protect her. First they describe her and then they ask a question about her—a question that has two possible answers. Here is what they sing:

> We have a little sister,
>   and she has no breasts.
> What shall we do for our sister
>   on the day when she is spoken for?
> If she is a wall,
>   we will build on her a battlement of silver,
> but if she is a door,
>   we will enclose her with boards of cedar. (8:8–9;
>   cf. 1:6)

The context for these lyrics is a culture in which most marriages were arranged. The brothers have a younger sister who is old enough to be promised in marriage but is not yet sexually mature. Today we might say that she was going through puberty. As her body develops its sexual characteristics, she has a choice to make, a choice that her brothers describe using two household images.

Maybe their sister will be an impenetrable wall. In other words, she may choose to protect her sexual purity, keeping her body safely within the confines of virginity until marriage. If this is the choice she makes, then her vigilant family will reward her with a generous dowry. "If she is a wall," they say, "we will build on her a battlement of silver."

On the other hand, their sister may turn out to be less like a solid wall and more like a door that swings loose, as it were, on its sexual hinges. So the choice is between chastity and promiscuity.

This choice is not just for little sisters, of course, either in the Bible or in everyday life. Here the Song of Songs speaks mainly to women. But the book of Proverbs typically counsels men on the subjects of lust and sexual purity (e.g., Prov. 6:20–35). We find the same thing in the psalms: "How can a young man keep his way pure? By guarding it according to your word" (Ps. 119:9). The application of all of these verses is for everyone, male or female. If we are wise, we will do everything we can to protect and promote sexual purity—both our own purity and the purity of others.

Some scholars accuse the brothers in the Song of Songs of being overbearing. It's one thing to guide your little sister with godly counsel, they say, but it's another thing to lock her in a closet. Besides, they speak *about* her rather than *to* her, which seems to show a lack of respect. She is someone "spoken for" (8:8) rather than someone who has a voice of her own. These scholars may be right, but since the brothers are speaking about doors and walls metaphorically, maybe we should give them some benefit of the doubt. They are trying to protect their sister from a harmful relationship, as family members should.

We need to be careful not to play God for other people, of course. But we are called to watch out for one another, and sometimes this includes helping people stay out of trouble sexually. In what we say and think, in what we look at and daydream about, in what we wear and what we touch, we should do what members of Wheaton College promise to do in the campus's Community Covenant: "uphold chastity among the unmarried and the sanctity of marriage between a man and a woman."

Having the Last Word

The woman we meet in the Song of Songs is an extraordinary example of surrendering sexuality to the glory of God. She is hardly a blushing bride. Her first song was about wanting to be kissed, and things only got more passionate from there. But she took personal and communal responsibility for her chastity. Her brothers need not have worried. She was careful to uphold her honor by maintaining proper sexual boundaries until finally she chose to marry the man of her dreams.

Was it worth it? Of course it was! The Scripture says, "Hope deferred makes the heart sick, but a desire fulfilled is a tree of life" (Prov. 13:12). In this case, the woman's testimony speaks for itself: "I was a wall, and my breasts were like towers; then I was in his eyes as one who finds peace" (Song 8:10). Here the bride uses the imagery that her brothers used and tells us plainly that she is a wall, not a door. She has no need for adornment; her body itself is beautiful. Furthermore, the way she describes her body indicates that she is as ready for sex as anyone. She is not a girl anymore; she's a woman!

At the same time, the lover in the Song of Songs wants us to know that she has saved herself for marriage so that she can bring peace to the man she loves. Sexual immorality always stirs up trouble, but sexual purity brings peace in the sense of wholeness or *shalom*. So does sexual repentance, in which we go straight to God with our sexual sins, ask him to make us pure again, and experience the peace of his forgiving, sanctifying grace. The great Welsh preacher Martyn Lloyd-Jones rightly said:

> Even adultery is not the unforgivable sin. It is a terrible sin, but God forbid that there should be anyone who feels that he or she has sinned himself or herself outside the love of God or outside His kingdom because of adultery. No, if you truly repent and realize the enormity of your sin and cast yourself upon the boundless love and mercy and grace of God, you can be forgiven and I assure you of pardon.[8]

None of this is what our culture says about sex, of course. Then again, I'm not sure it's ever been easy or popular to stay pure. In fact, as the bride in this song considered her commitment to chastity, with all its challenges, she could see a clear contrast between the choice she had made and the concubines of King Solomon. Here is how she described the difference:

> Solomon had a vineyard at Baal-hamon;
>   he let out the vineyard to keepers;
>   each one was to bring for its fruit a thousand pieces
>   of silver.

My vineyard, my very own, is before me;
you, O Solomon, may have the thousand,
and the keepers of the fruit two hundred. (8:11–12)

The word "vineyard" in these verses seems to be a metaphor for a woman's body. With seven hundred wives and three hundred concubines, Solomon had a thousand "vineyards." There were so many women in his harem that he had to hire people to look after them! But as far as the singer was concerned, the king could keep his thousand vineyards. She had only one garden to tend—the precious vineyard of her body—and one was enough for her.

These word pictures are meant to encourage us to pursue passion with purity. Honor God's call to care for your vineyard through modesty and chastity. Do not trample other people's grapes by pressuring them to share sexual intimacy or by taking advantage of them sexually. Do not spoil your vineyard by looking at pornography, which sets unrealistic expectations and is degrading to women especially. Instead, follow the example set in the Song of Songs, which is dripping with desire but also passionate about purity.

The woman in the Song of Songs wanted to offer her body as a pure gift to her beloved husband. So as their anthology of love songs comes to a close, we see the happy couple slipping off to the garden of love together, alone. We hear the man call out, "O you who dwell in the gardens, with companions listening for your voice; let me hear it" (8:13). He wants his lover to let him know where she is. Then she responds with an audible invitation to intimacy: "Make haste, my beloved, and be like a gazelle or a young stag on the mountains of spices" (8:14; cf. 2:17; 5:1).

The bride is speaking in metaphors again, but it is not hard to guess what she wants. The woman gets both the first word and the last word in the Song of Songs. When her song began, and she was still single, she wanted her man to hurry up and kiss her. Now that she's married, she's still in a hurry, but what she wants is more than a kiss. So the song ends with the happy couple moving toward sexual intimacy—not for the first time, and not for the last time either.

This is an extraordinary ending to the world's greatest love song. Many people would be surprised to learn that there is a book in the Bible that ends with somebody asking for sex. But under the inspiration of the Holy Spirit (!), the woman leaves us on the edge of desire, longing for satisfaction. We get the sense that their lovemaking will never end.

The Savior and the Bride Say, Come!

This is also the way the Bible ends, with a husband and a wife moving toward one another in total intimacy. At the end of the book of Revelation, in the very last words of Scripture, we meet a bride who says, "Come" (Rev. 22:17). She represents the church, waiting for the second coming of the Son of God, who is promised to her in marriage. Then she hears Jesus speak to her. Her beloved Savior says, "Surely I am coming soon." His bride can hardly wait. So she says in response, "Amen. Come, Lord Jesus!" (Rev. 22:20).

The bride and the groom at the end of Revelation are so close that they are almost touching—but not quite. Thus the end of the Bible leaves us on the edge of desire, waiting to be with our Savior, longing for intimacy with him, wanting to make spiritual love, ready to give ourselves to our loving Husband without holding anything back.

Jesus Christ is worthy of our every desire, because his love is everything we see in the Song of Songs, and more. Whether we are married or single, male or female, this is the love that we have always wanted and needed. Lean on Jesus—the way a bride leans on her beloved husband, or the way John leaned against his loving Lord Jesus at the Last Supper (John 13:23–25)—and he will support you through every trouble. Your Savior has set you as a seal upon his heart; his love will never leave you or forsake you. If you know Jesus by faith, then he has also placed his seal on you: the seal of the Holy Spirit, who is the guarantee of eternal life (2 Cor. 1:22; Eph. 1:13–14). You are his, and he is yours—forever.

The love of Jesus is as strong as death—no, stronger! He loved you all the way to death on the cross, but his love did not die in the grave. His death was the defeat of death, and therefore on the third day he rose again with the power of eternal love. His triumphant love for you can never be extinguished by any doubt, drowned by any sorrow, or quenched by any enemy, which means that the song of his love for you will never, ever end.

Epilogue

Happily Ever After

The battle is over. The enemy is defeated. The powers of darkness have been destroyed. And now the rightful king stands victorious on the battlefield.

This is the situation in *The Lord of the Rings* after King Aragorn and his armies have defeated the Dark Lord Sauron at the Gates of Mordor. But the story is not quite finished. Aragorn the conqueror is destined to enter the fair City of Minas Tirith, where he will be crowned as king and then married to the bride he has been waiting for all his life. So after the battle, "there in the midst of the fields they set up their pavilions and awaited the morning; for it was the Eve of May, and the King would enter his gates with the rising of the Sun."[1]

Aragorn's beautiful bride arrived some weeks later—Arwen, Evenstar, shimmering like the moonlight. The handsome groom and his fair bride were married at Midsummer. Then the royal couple lived happily ever after, and whenever people saw their king in the splendor of his majesty, they glimpsed a "glory undimmed before the breaking of the world."[2]

J. R. R. Tolkien said that he wrote these words to awaken our longing for "the return in majesty of the true King," who is Jesus Christ.[3] The images Tolkien used to tell his story were drawn from the last pages of the Bible, where a glorious king triumphs over his enemies and then enters a golden city to marry his long-awaited bride, "the wife of the Lamb," beautifully adorned for her husband (Rev. 21:2, 9). This is not just a great story; it is also our destiny. But to understand this, it helps to know the backstory.

Love Story

As we saw in the prologue to this book, the Bible begins with the marriage of a worthy man to a beautiful woman. In fact, they are the perfect couple—the only perfect couple in the history of the world. The first man and the first woman are introduced to one another by none other than God himself, who is the father of the bride. As soon as the man meets his match, he speaks poetically: "This at last is bone of my bones and flesh of my flesh" (Gen. 2:23). Then the Bible makes the world's first wedding announcement: "Therefore a man shall leave his father and his mother and hold fast to his wife, and they shall become one flesh" (Gen. 2:24).

Thus begins the love story that runs all the way through sacred Scripture. Marriage is a picture of God's faithful love for his beloved people. His eternal purpose is for us to be with and belong to his Son. Thus the Bible often uses the imagery of matrimony—both marital success and marital failure—to describe our on-again, off-again relationship with the living God. The mystery of marriage is one of the Bible's main metaphors for the romance of our redemption. We are fickle, but he is faithful, so against all odds, we are still together. New

York City's Tim Keller likes to say that God has been trapped in the longest bad marriage in history. But even when he had legitimate grounds for divorce, God never gave up on his people. This is all leading up to the happy day when the church of Jesus Christ will be presented as a perfect bride for the Son of God. We are like the holy bridesmaids in the story Jesus told about the groom who arrived at midnight. They waited late into the night, until finally they heard the happy news: "Here is the bridegroom! Come out to meet him!" (Matt. 25:6). Thus the Bible and human history both end the way they began: with a happy marriage under the blessing of a loving God. This romance is the ultimate reality.

We have been listening to the soundtrack for this love story throughout our study of the Song of Songs. This remarkable book tells us what kind of relationship God wants to have with us: passionate, affectionate, driven by holy desire. If this is what we want too, then one day we will be satisfied, because the book of Revelation gives this promise to the bride of Christ: "He will wipe away every tear from their eyes, and death shall be no more, neither shall there be mourning, nor crying, nor pain anymore, for the former things have passed away. And he who was seated on the throne said, 'Behold, I am making all things new'" (Rev. 21:4–5). And so they lived happily ever after. That's what this promise means. God will take everything negative—death, pain, tears, sorrow—and get rid of it forever. Happily, ever, after. But notice that the Bible never says, "The end," because this love song never will end.

The Next Chapter

The problem, of course, is that we are not there yet. All of us have received a wedding invitation from the longest guest list ever, drawn from people of every tribe, every tongue, and every nation. Hopefully we have returned our RSVP. We do this by saying yes to Jesus Christ. If we believe that Jesus died on the cross for our sins and rose again with the power of eternal life, then by faith we know there is a place for us at the wedding supper of the Lamb. This is one wedding that no one should miss, because it will be the best wedding ever—a wedding to end all weddings. It will have the proudest father: the Father God who rejoices in his only beloved Son and then presents to him a purified bride. It will have the worthiest groom with the heart of greatest love: Jesus Christ, who suffered and sacrificed more for his beloved bride than any other groom in the history of the world. What the Bible says is true: "Blessed are those who are invited to the marriage supper of the Lamb" (Rev. 19:9).

We are waiting for the happy nuptials, when the wedding guests will say, "'Let us rejoice and exult and give him the glory, for the marriage of the Lamb has come, and his Bride has made herself ready; it was granted her to clothe herself with fine linen, bright and pure'—for the fine linen is the righteous deeds of the saints" (Rev. 19:7–8). But that happy day seems so far off that sometimes we wonder if it will ever come. Indeed, we have been waiting longer for this wedding than for any other. Day after day after day, we are waiting for the last of all weddings, which will be followed by the best and biggest reception the world has ever witnessed. But in the meantime we continue to have all the struggles that Revelation talks about: death, mourning, crying, and pain. It is not "happily ever after" at all—far from it!

One way I know this is from the painful losses we suffer at Wheaton College. Our campus is full of life; our vibrant young students have their whole lives in front of them. But we also experience death. We witness tragic accidents, suffer the ravages of disease, and experience grief through the deaths of students, faculty, staff, and alumni. All too frequently, we are reminded of our mortality.

This world is not pain free. We see this in every community, not just at Wheaton College. We suffer painful conflicts over race, theology, and sexuality. People we care about leave and go far away. All of us get discouraged at one point or another. Some despair of life itself. We face major setbacks. We fail in areas where we really want to succeed. Our families have problems we never expected and have no idea how to solve. Relationships are broken and prove impossible to put together.

Given all this suffering, sometimes I tell my students that they are living somewhere east of Eden and south of the New Jerusalem. I desperately wish I could say that the next chapters of their story will be trouble-free, that they will never suffer pain or go through grief ever again, that twenty-two is forever. But I know that the world they are called to serve is every bit as fallen as the campus where they live, play, study, and worship. So the next chapter of their life story is likely to be much harder than they want it to be. They will not experience "no more crying" until after they get to the end of their pilgrimage. In the meantime, they will experience more death, more grief, more pain. Love stories are like that; usually they are bad in the middle and do not get really good until the end.

How Knowing the End Helps You Live the Middle

So what difference does knowing the end of the story make for living the middle? How does the *last* chapter influence the way we live the *next* chapter? If our life story ends "happily ever after," as the Bible says it does, then what implications does this have for chapters that have titles like, "The Day I Lost Everything," or, "When My Dream Became a Nightmare"?

It makes a massive difference to know that we are in the middle of a story that ends "happily ever after." First, knowing this truth teaches us not to be surprised by suffering.

There is an implicit contrast in Revelation 21:4. Here the Bible describes a scene from which evil is absent. Yet the very fact that it tells us there is no more death or pain in the New Jerusalem indicates something very important about our present experience. If we had already reached the place where there are no more tears, then the Bible wouldn't need to tell us about it. Obviously, then, we must still be living in a world of hurt.

Knowing the truth about our present sufferings helps us to have the right expectations. One of the reasons some people get disillusioned is that somehow they expect life to be perfect. If we are wise, however, we will not carry a sense of entitlement with us through life's changes. Instead, we will know that wherever we are right now, and wherever we are going next, we will suffer there too.

When things go wrong, as they certainly will, we should remember that we are not off script. Instead, we should realize that whatever we are going through was always going to be part of our story. There is no need to be angry, as if somehow God failed to live up to his part of the bargain. Sin brings suffering into the world, and there is no way for anyone to escape it. But our trials are only temporary. We will have more joys and more sorrows until our story takes its final turn—one last twist in the plot. Then there will be no more death and no more pain forever!

An inspiring example of how having the right expectations can empower someone to hold on to hope when everything seems lost comes from the sands of Africa. The year 2014 witnessed the appalling murder of twenty-one Egyptian Christians on a deserted beach in Libya. The young men—who were beheaded by soldiers from the Islamic State—had been in Libya to earn enough money to go back home and get married. When one of their fathers was asked about the martyrdom of his son, he offered a gospel perspective that anticipated the end of his son's story: "He left to marry heaven, where he'll meet Christ."[4]

Knowing who we will meet at the end of the story also gives us the courage to persevere through present trials. Sometimes it seems as if our suffering will never end. But we should not get too discouraged or slip into despair. We definitely shouldn't give up. Instead, we should flip ahead to the last chapter and remember how the story ends. Then we will realize that by the grace of God, we are going to make it to the last chapter. When we doubt we can take another step, when we don't think we can make it through even one more day, we should anticipate the final scene. There we can see ourselves standing with our Lover and Friend in the new heavens and the new earth. The vows that Jesus has made to us are not conditional. He has promised to love us no matter what and stay with us to the very end. Believing his promise will give us the courage to persevere through our present trials and live into our eternal destiny.

When we remember how the story ends, we have the hope to persevere. Dr. Jamie Aten, who teaches psychology at Wheaton College and directs the Humanitarian Disaster Institute, persevered through a life-or-death struggle with cancer. Aten survived his own "personal disaster" as he calls it, yet his surgeries also left him with significant scarring.

One day Dr. Aten's youngest daughter walked by his bedroom and saw him buttoning his shirt. He could see her reflection in the mirror as she paused to look at all the scars that the surgeon's blade had left behind. Softly she asked if he would still have his scars in heaven. "No, Sweetie," he said. "God will give Daddy a new body. There will be no more scars." As Dr. Aten's answer slowly sunk in, a huge smile formed on his daughter's face. "Yes!" she shouted. Then she gave him a fist bump and walked down the hall. Father and daughter—living into their destiny gave them the courage and the joy to face another day.

Here Comes the Groom!

Another way that knowing the end of the story helps us live the middle is by teaching without a doubt whom we can trust. The promises in the book of Revelation—promises about the death of death and the end of all our tears—are the personal commitments of Jesus Christ. The Bible is not speaking in abstractions here. There is a *he* in these verses—a real person who will be with us to help us. *He* will dwell with us. *He* will be our God. *He* will wipe away our tears. *He* will make all things new. When we finally see the new heavens and the new earth, the source of all our happiness will be the living presence of our loving Savior, Jesus Christ.

Try to imagine the moment when you finally enter the gates of heaven. There will still be tears on your cheeks, because right up until our last moments on this earth, we bear the sorrows of a fallen world—tears of frustration, tears of repentance and regret, tears of grief for the loved ones we have lost. But Jesus will be there to meet us, and with the handkerchief of his grace, he will reach out to wipe away the last tears we will ever shed.

When that day comes, we will not be meeting Jesus for the first time. Although we may be *seeing* him for the first time, we will know him already by faith, because he has promised to be with us every step of the way. The Lover who will be with us from the last chapter until forever is the same Friend who has loved us from the very beginning of our story.

Knowing that Jesus will be there loving us at the end helps us trust him right here and right now. He loves us so much that he will do whatever it takes to see us through. If we ever doubt this, all we need to do is go back to the gospel. There we see that the things Jesus has promised to take away from us—death and mourning and pain—are all things that he had to suffer for our salvation.

Jesus wept. He was "a man of sorrows, acquainted with deepest grief" (Isa. 53:3 NLT). He shed tears of sorrow at the tomb of his dear friend Lazarus (John 11:35, 38). He was moved with compassion for the lost souls of Israel (Matt. 9:36). During the days of his life on this earth, Jesus offered up "prayers and supplications, with loud cries and tears" (Heb. 5:7). In humbling himself to become human, the Son of God experienced all the grief of a suffering world, as these examples serve to illustrate.

Jesus also experienced pain—not only the excruciating physical pain of dying on the cross but also the emotional pain of personal betrayal and scornful ridicule, as well as being forsaken by his Father God. Jesus suffered these pains all the way to death and then down into the grave. Never forget that your Savior is the groom who paid the ultimate price for his bride. In the immortal words of Saint Ignatius, we are "the spouse of Christ, for whom, instead of a dowry, He poured out His own blood, that he might redeem her."[5]

Jesus endured it all—all the tears, all the pain, all the death. He did this so that he could take it all away from us, so that at the end of our story we would never suffer any of these things ever again. Jesus suffered what he suffered on our behalf, so that together with him we could live "happily ever after."

Knowing the tears Jesus shed and the pains he suffered means that we can trust him with everything we are going through today. Knowing that he has promised to put an end to all our trials means that we can also trust him for tomorrow. When we know how the story ends, we are ready to live more patiently, more courageously, more compassionately, and more hopefully.

The Last Chapter

One of my favorite examples of faithful perseverance is Lilias Trotter. Lilias was a gifted artist—so gifted that leading artists in Victorian England such as John Ruskin thought that she could become her nation's greatest living painter. Yet Miss Trotter believed that God had called her to depart from England and leave the art world behind in order to become a pioneer missionary to North Africa. Once she was clear about her calling, she said to the Lord, "I am now ready to be offered."[6]

Lilias Trotter went to the sands of Algeria as a single woman, not knowing a word of Arabic, ready to give all she had to the work of the gospel. Nothing about her life there was glamorous. She and her two coworkers faced many hardships, with little to show for their efforts. In her journal she wrote, "January was one of the darkest and toughest months we've ever had. One literally could do nothing but pray at every available moment. Still the light does not come. Just a blind holding on to a dim Christ."

Some would say that Lilias Trotter wasted her life. Yet in her beautiful life she was faithful to God's calling. She once wrote,

"Take the very hardest thing in your life—*the* place of difficulty, outward or inward, and expect God to triumph gloriously in that very spot. Just there He can bring your soul into blossom!" As she reflected on the hardships that she and her friends faced in Algeria, far from home and family, she also said, "Before us all dawned a new horizon, a glory in its every hardness and the sense we are working for its future and its coming day."

Lilias Trotter lived the middle of her life looking in hope to the end of her story. She knew Jesus Christ as the Lover of her soul, the Bridegroom of her salvation. When she came to her last day—the last page of the last chapter of her earthly life—her close friends gathered at her bedside. By their account, just before Lilias died she began to see visions of the new heavens and the new earth. When they asked her what she saw, she simply said, "Many beautiful things."

These were the last words that Lilias Trotter ever spoke in this world. But we know what happened next. It is the same thing that will happen to everyone who has a love relationship with Jesus Christ. Lilias Trotter married the Son of God and lived happily ever after, which is exactly the way a love story is supposed to end.

Acknowledgments

This little book began as a series of chapel messages given at Wheaton College during the 2015–2016 school year. The Song of Songs was an exciting book for us to hear together as a campus that year, as students from Wheaton's Arena Theater dramatized its text every month in word and song. It was also an exciting book to preach, with its intimate and sometimes smoldering portrayal of romance, love, marriage, and sex—more or less in that order.

Many words of thanks are needed. Mark Lewis organized the actors whose interpretation of the Song of Songs captivated our campus: Jessie Epstein, John Ingraham, Travis Shanahan, and Olivia Wilder. Lynn Cohick—who teaches New Testament at Wheaton and served as faculty vice-chair that year—made helpful comments and suggestions during the chapel series. Mary Ryken helped edit the first draft, as did Tom Schwanda, who teaches spiritual formation at the College. Lynn Wartsbaugh entered corrections and helped prepare the final manuscript. Jon Nielson drew from his pastoral work with college students at Wheaton and Princeton to prepare the study guide. Finally, Lydia Brownback added many deft touches during the final editorial process at Crossway.

I am deeply grateful for the unique gifts of each of these friends and also for the many people who pray regularly for Wheaton's chapel services. This book is the fruit of their labors as much as my own.

Discussion Guide

Prologue

The prologue points us to the main purpose of our journey into the ancient biblical book of the Song of Songs, the celebration of the loving and committed relationship of human marriage, which points us to the deeper—and more permanent—loving relationship between Christians and their Savior.

Discussion Starter

Have you studied the Song of Songs in the past? If so, what have been some of your struggles or difficulties in reading and/or applying it? If you haven't read it or studied it before, what are some of the frequent comments you've heard about it?

Where have you heard the best teaching about marriage? What questions do you have about marriage and its place in God's plan?

Observation and Analysis

1. Why is it important to understand and read this book not only as God's Word but also as poetry? What might we miss if we totally ignore the poetic elements?

2. How will this book seek to read the Song of Songs not a mere allegory but as truly pointing beyond itself to the gospel? Why is this important for our study?

3. How did the prologue enlarge and expand your view of the significance of human marriage? What did you learn about God's concern for human marriage?

4. What does human marriage teach us about the salvation and love that Jesus has for his people? How does marriage (and adultery) imagery in the Bible teach us about sin and spiritual unfaithfulness?

5. Regardless of your relational situation (single, dating, newly married, married for a long time, widowed, or divorced), how can the deep love of God for sinful people be seen through the poetic pictures of the Song of Songs?

Reflection and Action

1. How should the deep importance of human marriage (both to God, and as a picture of God's love) shape the way you think about marriage? How do you need to change, expand, or adjust the way you view human marriage?

2. In what ways does the Bible's vision for human marriage collide with our culture's view on marriage? How can you push back, from God's Word, toward a biblical vision for marriage?

3. Take some time to consider how the marriage images throughout Scripture (in the gospel, in the spiritual adultery of God's people, and in the final wedding day of Revelation) can help you better understand your relationship with your

Savior. How are these helpful for you, specifically, in your stage of life and relational status?

Additional Options for Discussion Leaders

Consider gathering some quotations, words of advice, or pointers about romance and marriage from broader secular culture and reading those at the beginning. Then contrast some of these with the heart of this prologue (the picture of marriage throughout Scripture representing God's salvation of his adulterous people, who are graciously wed to a Savior who will love them forever).

Chapter 1: You're the One That I Want

The scene has been set for our study of the Song of Songs; it's a wedding, complete with feasting, dancing, and celebrating the love of a young, excited couple. This couple is obviously growing in their affection, admiration, and mutual desire for each other; they say so, expressing their love, desire, and anticipation of their married relationship together, in the context of the faith community that surrounds them.

Discussion Starter

Talk about some of the basic cultural assumptions about love, sex, and romance held by those in the place where you live. What does pop culture tell you? What do celebrities model for you? What basic messages about love, sex, and romance do some of your favorite movies or songs preach to you?

Observation and Analysis

1. If the Song of Songs had been written by King Solomon, what might that tell us about the kinds of lessons he

learned over the years? See page 30 and the reminder there about Solomon's own sinful and foolish choices in love and marriage.

2. Why is reading the Song of Songs in its proper context (covenant marriage) so important? What mistakes might we make, as readers, if we don't do this?

3. How does thinking of this biblical book as a "love song" help you as a reader?

4. As you consider the words of the bride, which are filled with desire, anticipation, and purpose, how do they help you understand biblical womanhood and femininity? What do you learn about this young, strong, godly woman?

5. How do you see the man affirming the woman in this chapter? What can young Christian men learn today from his words?

6. How does this chapter connect what is happening between the man and the woman (moving closer to each other in love and admiration) to the message of the gospel of Jesus Christ and the love of God for his people?

Reflection and Action

1. "The Song of Songs aches with sexual desire, but it surrenders sex to the glory of God by securing the satisfaction of its desire within the bridal chamber" (p. 30). Why is this combination so radically countercultural? What are some ways that you might grow in winsomely representing this sexual ethic to the world around you?

2. What do you learn from the woman's words about her self-image struggles? How can Christians lead the way in guiding others toward healthy self-image as well as the pursuit of affirmation in the right places?

3. How can Christian men take the lead today in setting a new biblical standard for talk about women? For you, young men, how can *you* make a Christ-focused commitment to affirm your sisters in Christ?

4. In what ways do you need to intentionally reorder your desires to ensure that your deepest longings are directed toward God first and foremost? How and why do your desires sometimes get misdirected? How can we fight this?

Additional Options for Discussion Leaders

Considering that this chapter focuses on the back-and-forth dialogue between a young couple that is growing in affection, desire, and romance, you could talk more about the role of conversation in a guy/girl relationship, and specifically a dating relationship. What ought to be guiding principles for followers of Jesus who seek to date with purity, care, and intentionality? What are appropriate expressions of admiration, respect, and love—and why?

Chapter 2: Underneath the Apple Tree

Chapter 2 takes us to the love-filled communication of the man and the woman as they express their desire for each other. Their passionate words are chastened, though, by a passionate commitment to God's plan for purity. There is desire, which is good! But there is also an appreciation and a love for the beauty of waiting. For us today, this waiting is linked to a faith-filled hope that our satisfaction and joy will ultimately be found in God alone.

Discussion Starter

"We were made to be lovers" (p. 44). What do you think about that comment? Does it strike you as true? What evidence do you find of its truth in the world around you and in your own life and heart?

Observation and Analysis

1. Our "desire for intimacy . . . can be satisfied only by a personal relationship with the living God" (p. 44). Why might this truth burst the bubble of some people who have made an idol of romance or marriage? Why is it freeing and empowering for Christians? Why might it actually lead to more joy in human marriage?

2. What do you learn from the repeated expressions of love that the couple in the passage give to each other? How is this an important lesson for human marriage? Why do we need to hear it again and again?

3. What desire seems to be behind the woman's words, as she responds to the man? How is this desire true of many women, and how does it point to a deeper desire that is meant to be satisfied ultimately in God?

4. How is the teaching on sexual intimacy contained in this part of the Song of Songs (wait to awaken sexual desire until marriage) not an example of God simply refusing to give us something good? What is the good that God has for us in this command? How is he after our deeper pleasure?

5. In what ways must we go back to Jesus, both as our example in purity and as our gracious Savior when we fail?

Reflection and Action

1. In what ways might you be guilty of not pursuing and enjoying intimacy with Jesus? How are you living as a spiritual single, and how might you pray and work to change that?

2. What do the woman's words to the man say to men about what godly women are looking for? Men, how might this part of the Song of Songs shape your goals as a follower of Jesus Christ or as a future husband? Women, how might these verses reshape some of what you tend to look for in a man?

3. Why is "patience before passion" (p. 53) such an important lesson for Christian young people to hear? What gets in the way of that earnest message, given by the young woman on the eve of her wedding night? What other messages drown out that warning, and how can we fight them?

4. How can the person of Jesus be more central to you in your pursuit of sexual purity at this point in your life?

Additional Options for Discussion Leaders

This would be a good place to talk about desires in relationships. What are good ones? What are bad ones? How can these desires get out of line when a relationship with Jesus is not central (e.g., a woman's desire for security, which is mentioned in this chapter, or a man's desire for a woman who represents physical beauty)?

Chapter 3: I'm for You, and You're for Me

The lover continues his pursuit of the beloved as images of springtime permeate this section of the Song of Songs. Yet the beloved again answers with chastity and a caution toward the importance of sexual purity, even as their desire for each other increases. They don't say "never" to sexual intimacy; they say "not yet." A godly couple continues to respect the passion of sexual intimacy and to wait for its God-ordained context: holy marriage.

Discussion Starter

"You are the bride of Christ." You've probably heard this phrase before. It's directed to the church of Jesus Christ as a metaphor. What is your initial reaction to that metaphor? Has it been helpful for you or problematic or confusing? Discuss this together.

Observation and Analysis

1. In what ways does the love and pursuit of the bridegroom for his soon-to-be bride teach us about Jesus's passionate love for his people? Why is the message that we are loved with an everlasting love such an important one for young people to hear today?

2. If the woman, in her response to the man, is truly making a statement about the importance of safeguarding sexual purity, what can we learn from this? Why should young Christian men and women involve "the assistance and oversight of people who know what they are doing" in their dating relationships (p. 70)?

3. Where and how do we see the strength of the young woman in the passages covered in this chapter? How is she an example of strength, commitment, and independence?

4. How does the gospel remind us that there is grace for us, even when we fail in areas of sexual sin? In what ways does the hope of Jesus Christ give us power and hope for a fresh start, for new commitments to holiness and sexual purity?

5. Why is it so important that we see our sexuality as linked to our relationship with God? What does it tell us about our God, that he created sexuality yet asks us to guard it and put it in its proper place?

Reflection and Action

1. What dangers in dating do you think could be avoided by carefully and intentionally involving godly older people in our relationships? How can you make a commitment to date in public, with the involvement of mature people whom you trust? Older couples, how might you have a role to play in dating relationships of younger couples in your community?

2. Why do you think young women find it hard to "send away" men's physical and sexual advances that come before marriage? What are some of the pressures on both men and women that get in the way of a firm commitment to sexual purity?

3. What might it look like for young Christian men and women (including you, yourself) to make a new commitment to "dedicate our sexuality to God" (p. 76)? How can the context of Christian community give support and encouragement to that kind of dedication? How does this commitment change

as we grow older, either in the context of marriage or of singleness? How does it remain the same?

Additional Options for Discussion Leaders

A major theme in this chapter is the importance of the context of Christian community in dating relationships, the involvement of older, godly, wise people (including parents!) who can give counsel, instruction, and accountability to a young dating couple. This would be a good chapter from which to do a thought experiment, considering some of the ways that young dating couples could more intentionally invite this kind of involvement from the church into their relationships. Such involvement would certainly be countercultural, but it's so important for relationships that are headed toward godly marriage.

For older couples, or couples who have experienced at least several years of marriage, one topic for further examination would be God's role for them in the lives of younger dating couples. What could mentoring look like? How could married couples in the church, for example, supplement the pastor's role of premarital counseling, conversation, and preparation for marriage?

Chapter 4: Royal Wedding

We've finally arrived. The passionate romance, which has included both desire and disciplined restraint, has made its way to marriage. Celebration abounds in a picture of the glorious wedding feast of man and woman, and also Savior and bride. Sexual intimacy finally arrives, and the bride and groom enjoy each other's bodies but also their mutual love. It's a deep love and intimacy that points us to the greatest fulfillment of all our desires in our Savior God.

Discussion Starter

Talk about weddings. What are the focal points of most weddings in today's culture? How are they portrayed in movies and songs? What do people tend to talk about the most? What elements of weddings can get lost in the mix, at least from a Christian perspective?

Observation and Analysis

1. In what ways have we been seeing a progression in the love songs of the Song of Songs? Identify the different steps and how they have led finally to the point of the wedding and the wedding night.

2. How does this part of the Song of Songs show us the bridegroom joyfully celebrating his bride? Why is this a good thing? How does this point to something even deeper for followers of Jesus Christ?

3. The explanation of sexual love within the context of marriage is focused on mutual belonging, ownership, passion, and surrender. How is this helpful to you? Why is this biblical picture of sex so damaged by sexual relationships outside the bounds of marriage?

4. What are some ways that single people (either not yet married or never married) can learn from God's plan for sex? What can a commitment to sexual purity or celibacy teach about God and his love?

5. Without allowing the metaphor of marriage to become overly graphic, how does love, and even sexual intimacy, ultimately point us to God and his love for his people? Why *must* we see

Jesus Christ as the ultimate fulfillment of all our desires, even desires for intimacy?

Reflection and Action

1. How can an appreciation of the beauty and purpose of sex help guide our commitment to guard it for marriage? In what ways have you heard weaker arguments for sexual purity, those that don't sufficiently consider God's beautiful purpose for sex?

2. Why is it so important for young people to see sex as not "only about bodies" but about "whole persons" (p. 92)? When sex becomes just about physical pleasure, what is lost, from God's perspective? What problems does a body-only view of sex create?

3. Think about the phase of life you are in right now: single; single but dating; engaged; married. What are some steps that you can take—right now—to better celebrate and protect God's plan for sexual intimacy and its relationship to the gospel of his Son? How can you encourage others to do the same?

Additional Options for Discussion Leaders

A major point in this chapter is the way our culture has brought sex out into the open rather than kept it gloriously hidden and contained in the context of the marriage bedroom. In what ways has our culture actually cheapened sex, even as it is an idol to so many today? Discuss the way that God's view and design for sex is actually much higher than that of a culture that has allowed it to spill over into every part of life.

Chapter 5: Lovers' Quarrel

The next section of the Song of Songs takes us into conflict, as the newlyweds have their first big fight. Things get ugly as expectations and desires don't line up; a period of brokenness and distance comes between this young couple. Ultimately, though, the covenantal commitment of holy marriage leads them toward resolution, in a beautiful picture of God's covenantal love toward his people through his Son, Jesus.

Discussion Starter

Have you ever dealt with a major conflict in a relationship? How did you deal with it? What did you learn from it? Why might learning how to deal Christianly with conflict be a great tool for preparing for a marriage that lasts?

Observation and Analysis

1. How does the lovers' quarrel take a turn toward darkness, and even danger? What factors lead to this? Consider the actions of both the man and the woman. What can you learn from this as you consider your own current, or future, relationships?

2. In what ways does the foundational commitment and covenant of marriage lead the way for conflict resolution? How do the young woman's vows shape her approach to the strain in their relationship?

3. In what ways does the theme of friendship emerge in the context of this loving relationship, even in the midst of conflict? Why is this category, friendship, so important for young Christians as they think about dating and marriage?

4. What factors seem to lead the couple back together? What role do their friends seem to play in this part of their story?

5. How can a loving, gracious, imperfect yet long-suffering human relationship give illustration to the love of Jesus for his sinful people? How must the love and sacrifice of Jesus shape every relationship we have, particularly the relationship of marriage?

Reflection and Action

1. In what ways have "patterns of selfishness" hurt or shaped past relationships in your life (p. 104)? How can you move forward, through Christ, to fighting and battling those patterns of selfishness?

2. How might false or unrealistic expectations prove problematic for Christian dating relationships, or even marriage? Identify some ways that Christian community and the truth of the Bible can help us form realistic expectations for dating and marriage.

3. What biblical truths do you absolutely need to grasp in order to form a healthy dating, and then marriage, relationship? Why is an understanding of sin, grace, forgiveness, and the gospel so important?

Additional Options for Discussion Leaders

This would be a good place for a deeper conversation about conflict in dating and marriage relationships. What, generally, causes conflict? How do false expectations play a role? What are some healthy (and biblical) responses to conflict? How can young people prepare realistically to do life with another sinful person in the context of marriage?

Chapter 6: The Duet after the Fight

After the fight discussed in the last chapter, the lovers engage in not only forgiveness but also reconciliation. The man pursues the woman again, not only physically but with words of affirmation and love. The enjoyment of sexual intimacy proves to be a bond for this couple as they seek to move on from the conflict in peace and toward fruitfulness in their marriage. Through their intimacy and self-giving love, we are again pointed to the amazing, intimate, and self-giving love of our crucified and risen Savior.

Discussion Starter

Have you ever experienced a really big fight with your parents? Your friend? Your boyfriend or girlfriend? Your husband or wife? What were the key things that needed to happen to make up? What partial apologies along the way proved to be insufficient? What actually must occur for a relationship to be made truly right?

Observation and Analysis

1. How is the distinction drawn between forgiveness and reconciliation helpful? Why is the pursuit of reconciliation so important for Christian relationships? How can this reflect Christ and the gospel?

2. In what ways do we find out that the man and the woman have actually achieved reconciliation, not merely one-sided forgiveness? How does the man prove to be a model of relational reconciliation for all men?

3. What connections between human marriage and the "marriage" of the church to Christ are made on page 122? Why is it essential for Christians to understand the "double meaning" of the Song of Songs and of marriage itself?

4. What role does sexual intimacy seem to play in conflict resolution, and even in the way forward, for the married couple? What does this teach you about the place and role of sex within marriage? How does this further remind us that sex must be guarded for marriage?

5. How does the "duet" (p. 128) teach us about the breadth and depth of a marriage relationship? What aspects of the relationship, and of the marriage, are celebrated here? In what ways is the biblical picture of a fruitful marriage so much richer than some of the pictures of marriage we see in our culture today?

6. How can sexual desire be a pathway that ultimately points us to Jesus? How does his gospel shape our need to be reconciled to those around us?

Reflection and Action

1. Do you have a history of broken relationships or serious conflict in relationships? How have you at times not pursued and achieved reconciliation? How can a love for Jesus motivate you to do that more intentionally?

2. How have you been guilty, at times, of cheapening sex (either in your mind or imagination or in reality)? How can this chapter help you to grow in your understanding of the

depth and importance of sex, even as the glue for a marriage relationship?

3. What aspects of matrimony do you need to think about more when it comes to considering "God's multiple purposes for marriage" (p. 131)? What aspects of dating and marriage do you tend to focus on most? What do you tend to miss? How can God's Word and God's gospel fill out your view of God's plan for marriage?

4. What do we learn from the fact that our God is pro-sex and the very one who created the gift of sex? In what ways do lesser forms of sexual enjoyment (masturbation, pornography, imaginative lust) actually hinder God's glorious pro-sex plan and vision? How can you seek God's plan with more passion and purity today?

Additional Options for Discussion Leaders

This chapter, which is the one focused most directly and heavily on God's plan and gift of sex within marriage, could lead to a more specific conversation about the dangers that occur when sex is ripped out of its proper context. This could involve a discussion about premarital sex, of course, but also about lust, pornography, masturbation, and sexual fantasy—all of which cheapen sex by focusing on one element of sex (e.g., visual, physical, mental).

Chapter 7: Forever Yours

This chapter brings us to the true "climax" of the romantic relationship we have been following through this book: not the wedding night but the covenantal love that continues for the rest of the married couple's lives. Their love will blossom, grow, and establish deeper and deeper roots as love leads to children, family, and life together. As this permanent relationship is held up as the Christian standard, the need for sexual purity and virginity (and the protection of these) is held out as a proper pursuit for lovers of God.

Discussion Starter

If you asked some of your friends, "What does true love look like?" what answers might you get? How would you begin answering this question, in light of this study in the Song of Songs? How is the picture of marital and covenantal love given to us in this book bigger, better, stronger, and deeper than some of the substitutes for true love that we see in culture and entertainment today?

Observation and Analysis

1. "The climax of their love story is not sexual but relational" (p. 136). How does this statement challenge some of today's assumptions about romantic love? How should this truth shape your approach to thinking about romantic relationships, and marriage as well?

2. How does Song of Songs 8:6–7 get us close to the author's definition of love? How is this definition helpful as you consider the true meaning of love?

3. How does God factor into the definition of love given in the Song of Songs? How *must* God factor into our definitions of love? Why is this so necessary?

4. What do we learn from the "guarding" language used by the siblings about protecting their young sister? What does this

chapter have to teach us about chastity, purity, and even the importance of virginity before marriage?

5. In what ways must Christians connect sexual purity to the gospel of Jesus Christ, rather than viewing it as simply an unfeeling standard of morality or a set of rules?

6. What do we learn from the bride's final words and her sense that her waiting was worth it? How does the beautiful picture of a bride adorned for her husband (to be loved by him alone) point us to the deepest and most beautiful truths of the gospel of Jesus Christ?

Reflection and Action

1. How should you respond to God, as you consider him afresh as the maker and designer of human sexuality and all that it leads to?

2. In what ways have you seen the culture around you separate sex from marriage? How can you, personally and in community, help to bind sex back to marriage in a God-centered and joyful way?

3. What would you say to someone who makes the claim that the Christian sexual ethic is for prudes, old-fashioned types, and boring people who are against having any fun?

4. The brothers of the young sister mentioned in this section of the Song of Songs serve almost as her sexual protectors. In what ways can you be a protector of sexual purity for Christian brothers and sisters? What would this look like for you personally? What can it look like in Christian community?

Additional Options for Discussion Leaders

This chapter, with its focus on chastity, purity, virginity, and even the protective nature of the older brothers who speak about their younger sister, can lead to some good discussion about the importance of accountability in the context of Christian community, as well as practical ways to begin these kinds of accountability relationships and conversations.

Epilogue: Happily Ever After

As this study in the Song of Songs concludes, we consider the way that every human love story is meant to point us to the great love story, the epic tale of the God who pursues, redeems, weds, and covenants with a sinful people whom he makes beautiful forever. Our beautiful destiny is coming, but we are not there yet. In the meantime we wait for the great wedding feast of the Lamb. As we wait, anticipating the great end to our love story gives us hope, courage, and joy, even in the midst of sufferings along the way.

Discussion Starter

Think and talk about "happily ever after." Why do fairy tales, love stories, and romantic movies tend to end with this idea? Does it ever happen in real life? What gets in the way of "happily ever after" in some people's lives and in some human love stories?

Observation and Analysis

1. Why can it be helpful to see the entire story of Scripture as a kind of love story? How does this expand your view of God and his saving work? How can this make better sense and meaning of human love stories, which echo God's great love story?

2. What grounds our hope, as Christians, that the story we are in will end "happily ever after" (p. 182)? How does the ending of the Christian story make sense of and bring hope in the difficult middle of the story?

3. In what way can the hope of seeing Jesus face-to-face more powerfully shape our daily lives? How can the *groom* imagery of Jesus help us with our imagining, and hoping for, this moment?

4. Why is it so important for us in the middle of the story to know that our Savior and Groom is one who wept and experienced terrible pain? How can the marriage imagery about Jesus expand our understanding of his love for his bride, for whom he paid the ultimate price?

5. What is striking, encouraging, or challenging to you about the closing story of Lilias Trotter? How can you learn from the simple faith, courage, and hope of this woman?

Reflection and Action

1. How do you need to let the ultimate love story of God and his people better shape your perspective on human love stories, even your own (present or future)? In what ways should a vision of the end help guide you in a dating relationship today?

2. What in your life and relationships reminds you that we are not there yet, when it comes to the conclusion of the perfect love story? Why must we remember where we are, in a fallen world, even as we pursue loving relationships?

3. How is the picture of Jesus as not only God and Savior but also lover and friend encouraging to you? In what ways can you

remind yourself daily about these aspects of Jesus's love and commitment to you as his follower?

Additional Options for Discussion Leaders

As you close this epilogue and the discussions and study of the Song of Songs, it would be good to talk practically about what difference this study will make in your lives. How will this great gospel love story make sense of every human love story? How will Jesus shape your approach to singleness, your dating relationship, or your marriage? How will hope and anticipation of the happy ending give you strength and courage in the midst of suffering?

Notes

Prologue

1. Raymond C. Ortlund Jr., *God's Unfaithful Wife: A Biblical Theology of Spiritual Adultery*, New Studies in Biblical Theology (Downers Grove, IL: InterVarsity, 1996), 171.
2. Ibid., 172.
3. Charlotte Brontë, *Jane Eyre* (New York: Barnes & Noble, 1993), 462.
4. Ray Ortlund Jr.'s book *God's Unfaithful Wife: A Biblical Theology of Spiritual Adultery*, provides a comprehensive overview of this theme in biblical theology.
5. Ortlund, *God's Unfaithful Wife*, 164.
6. Karl Barth, *The Doctrine of Creation*, vol. 3.1, *Church Dogmatics*, ed. G. W. Bromiley and T. F. Torrance (Edinburgh: T&T Clark, 1956–1975), 318.
7. Iain M. Duguid, *Song of Songs*, Reformed Expository Commentary (Phillipsburg, NJ: P&R, 2016), 9.

Chapter 1: You're the One That I Want

1. Pico Iyer, "The Song of Songs," *Portland* (Autumn 2015): 23.
2. Doug O'Donnell, *The Song of Solomon: An Invitation to Intimacy*, Preaching the Word (Wheaton, IL: Crossway, 2012), 19.
3. See Michael V. Fox, *The Song of Songs and the Ancient Egyptian Love Songs* (Madison, WI: University of Wisconsin Press, 1985), 97.
4. Duane A. Garrett, *Song of Songs*, Word Biblical Commentary 23b (Nashville, TN: Thomas Nelson, 2004), 128.
5. O'Donnell, *Song of Solomon*, 28.
6. Iain M. Duguid, *Song of Songs*, Reformed Expository Commentary (Phillipsburg, NJ: P&R, 2016), 4.
7. Iain M. Duguid, *The Song of Songs*, Tyndale Old Testament Commentaries 19 (Downers Grove, IL: InterVarsity, 2015), 83.
8. Garrett, *Song of Songs*, 145.
9. Cyril of Alexandria, quoted in Duguid, *Song of Songs*, xvi.

10. Duguid, *Song of Songs*, xvi.
11. Raymond C. Ortlund Jr., *God's Unfaithful Wife: A Biblical Theology of Spiritual Adultery*, New Studies in Biblical Theology (Downers Grove, IL: InterVarsity, 1996), 167.
12. Rabbi Saadia, quoted in O'Donnell, *Song of Solomon*, 15.

Chapter 2: Underneath the Apple Tree

1. Pico Iyer, "The Song of Songs," *Portland* (Autumn 2015): 22.
2. Nicholas of Lyra, *The Postilla of Nicholas of Lyra on the Song of Songs*, trans. James George Kiecker, Reformation Texts with Translation (1350–1650), ed. Kenneth Hagen (Milwaukee: Marquette University Press, 1998), 29.
3. Iain M. Duguid, *Song of Songs*, Reformed Expository Commentary (Phillipsburg, NJ: P&R, 2016), 11.
4. Augustine, *The Confessions of St. Augustine*, trans. Rex Warner (New York: New American Library, 1963), 235.
5. Doug O'Donnell, *The Song of Solomon: An Invitation to Intimacy*, Preaching the Word (Wheaton, IL: Crossway, 2012), 37.
6. Billy Joel, "Tell Her About It," *An Innocent Man* album, producer Phil Ramone (New York: Columbia Records, 1983).
7. "I Feel Pretty," *West Side Story*, producer, Jerome Robbins, et al., music by Leonard Bernstein, lyrics by Stephen Sondheim (1957).
8. Iain M. Duguid, *The Song of Songs*, Tyndale Old Testament Commentaries 19 (Downers Grove, IL: InterVarsity, 2015), 90.
9. Ibid., 90.
10. Michael V. Fox, *The Song of Songs and the Ancient Egyptian Love Songs* (Madison, WI: University of Wisconsin Press, 1985), 110.
11. C. S. Lewis, *Mere Christianity* (London: Geoffrey Bles, 1952), 95.
12. Donna Freitas, quoted in Mona Charen, "What the Left and Right Don't Get about Campus Rape," *The Federalist* (August 31, 2015), http://thefederalist.com/2015/08/31/what-the-left-and-right-dont-get-about-campus-rape/.
13. Kevin Miller, "Consistent Sexual Sacrifice," *Christianity Today: Leadership Journal* (October 5, 2015), https://www.christianitytoday.com/pastors/2015/fall/consistent-sexual-sacrifice.html.
14. Paul Tripp, "The Way of the Wise: Teaching Teenagers about Sex," *Journal of Biblical Counseling* 13, no. 3 (1995): 39–41.
15. Elisabeth Elliot, *Passion and Purity* (Grand Rapids, MI: Revell, 2002), 90.
16. Augustine, "Prayer of Petition," http://thespiritlife.net/facets/process/53-disciplined/disciplined-publications/4740-prayer-of-petition-by-st-augustine.

Chapter 3: I'm for You, and You're for Me

1. C. S. Lewis, *The Lion, the Witch and the Wardrobe* (London: Geoffrey Bles, 1950).
2. S. J. Stone, "The Church's One Foundation," 1866.
3. Iain M. Duguid, *The Song of Songs*, Tyndale Old Testament Commentaries 19 (Downers Grove, IL: InterVarsity Press, 2015), 98–99.
4. Pico Iyer, "The Song of Songs," *Portland* (Autumn 2015): 22.
5. C. S. Lewis, *Mere Christianity* (London: Geoffrey Bles, 1952), 102–3.
6. Thérèse of Lisieux, *The Autobiography of Saint Therese: The Story of a Soul*, trans. John Beevers (New York: Doubleday, 2001), 41.

Chapter 4: Royal Wedding

1. Leland Ryken, *The Literature of the Bible* (Grand Rapids, MI: Zondervan, 1974), 225.
2. See also 2:17, where the woman uses similar imagery to say that it is not yet time to make love.
3. Doug O'Donnell, *The Song of Solomon: An Invitation to Intimacy*, Preaching the Word (Wheaton, IL: Crossway, 2012), 81.
4. Iain M. Duguid, *Song of Songs*, Reformed Expository Commentary (Phillipsburg, NJ: P&R, 2016), 86.
5. Thomas Gledhill, *The Message of the Song of Songs*, The Bible Speaks Today (Downers Grove, IL: InterVarsity, 1994), 147.
6. C. S. Lewis, *Mere Christianity* (London: Geoffrey Bles, 1952), 98.
7. Barry Danylak, *A Biblical Theology of Singleness* (London: Grove, 2007), 3.
8. Ibid., 4. See also Barry Danylak, *Redeeming Singleness: How the Storyline of Scripture Affirms the Single Life* (Wheaton, IL: Crossway, 2010).
9. Dan B. Allender and Tremper Longman III, *Intimate Allies: Rediscovering God's Design for Marriage and Becoming Soul Mates for Life* (Wheaton, IL: Tyndale, 1995), 213.
10. Raymond C. Ortlund Jr., *God's Unfaithful Wife: A Biblical Theology of Spiritual Adultery*, New Studies in Biblical Theology (Downers Grove, IL: InterVarsity, 1996), 173.
11. Rusty Blazenhoff, "Wedding Dress Made from WWII Parachute That Saved Husband's Life," laughingsquid.com, July 14, 2011, https://laughingsquid.com/wedding-dress-made-from-wwii-parachute-that-saved-husbands-life/.

Chapter 5: Lovers' Quarrel

1. William Shakespeare, *A Midsummer Night's Dream*, 1.1.
2. Samuel J. Stone, "The Church's One Foundation," 1866.

Chapter 6: The Duet after the Fight

1. Nadine Collier, quoted in David Von Drehle, et al., "How Do You Forgive a Murder?" *Time* (June 2015), http://time.com/time-magazine-charleston-shooting-cover-story/.
2. Iain M. Duguid, *The Song of Songs*, Tyndale Old Testament Commentaries 19 (Downers Grove, IL: InterVarsity Press, 2015), 138.
3. Ibid., 137.
4. Ibid., 141.
5. Dietrich Bonhoeffer, cited in Timothy George, "Same-Self Marriage" *First Things* (November 17, 2014), http://www.firstthings.com/web-exclusives/2014/11/same-selfmarriage.

Chapter 7: Forever Yours

1. David B. Calhoun, *Princeton Seminary, vol. 2: The Majestic Testimony, 1869–1929* (Edinburgh: Banner of Truth, 1996), 315–16. See also Roger Nicole, "B. B. Warfield and the Calvinist Revival," *Great Leaders of the Christian Church*, ed. John D. Woodbridge (Chicago: Northfield, 1999), 344–46.
2. B. B. Warfield, quoted in Ned Stonehouse, *J. Gresham Machen: A Biographical Memoir* (Grand Rapids, MI: Eerdmans, 1954), 220.
3. C. S. Lewis, *The Four Loves* (New York: Harcourt Brace, 1988), 35.
4. Bruce Lee, *Artist of Life*, ed. John Little (Boston: Tuttle, 1999), 96.
5. Mona Charen, "What the Left and Right Don't Get about Campus Rape," *The Federalist* (August 31, 2015), http://thefederalist.com/2015/08/31/what-the-left-and-right-dont-get-about-campus-rape/.
6. Peggy Orenstein, "How Porn Is Changing a Generation of Girls," *Time* (March 30, 2016), http://time.com/4277523/girls-sex-women-porn/.
7. Iain M. Duguid, *The Song of Songs*, Tyndale Old Testament Commentaries 19 (Downers Grove, IL: InterVarsity Press, 2015), 155.
8. Martyn Lloyd-Jones, *Studies in the Sermon on the Mount* (Grand Rapids, MI: Eerdmans, 1984), 261.

Epilogue

1. J. R. R. Tolkien, *The Return of the King*, part 3, *The Lord of the Rings* (New York: Houghton Mifflin, 1993), 936.
2. J. R. R. Tolkien, "Here Follows a Part of the Tale of Aragorn and Arwen," in *The Return of the King* (New York: Houghton Mifflin, 1993), 1038.
3. J. R. R. Tolkien, *The Letters of J. R. R. Tolkien*, ed. Humphrey Carpenter (New York: Houghton Mifflin, 2000), 160.
4. Cited in Jamie Dean, "Unconquered," *WORLD* (December 12, 2015), 44.
5. Saint Ignatius, cited in John Owen, *The Works of John Owen*, 16 vols, ed. William H. Goold (New York: Robert Carter, 1852), 10:422.

6. All Lilias Trotter quotes come from the 2016 film *Many Beautiful Things*, produced by Hisao Kurosawa and distributed by Oxvision Films. See also I. Lilias Trotter, *Parables of the Cross* (London: Marshall Brothers, 1890); and *A Blossom in the Desert: Reflections of Faith in the Art and Writings of Lilias Trotter*, ed. Miriam Huffman Rockness (Grand Rapids, MI: Discovery, 2007).

General Index

Scripture Index

Also Available from Phil Ryken

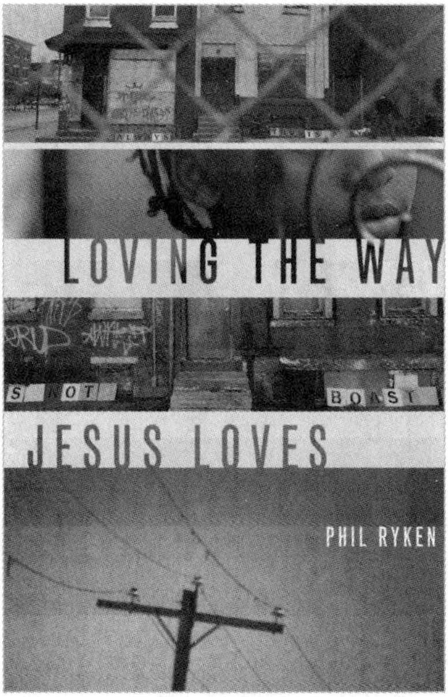

"A masterful, accessible exposition."

TIMOTHY J. KELLER

Best-selling author, The Reason for God

"This book will almost certainly challenge your presuppositions about love and help you see authentic love in a whole new light."

JOHN MACARTHUR

Pastor, Grace Community Church, Sun Valley, California;
President, The Master's University and Seminary

"This is a gift to the entire church."

R. ALBERT MOHLER JR.

President, The Southern Baptist Theological Seminary

For more information, visit **crossway.org**.